Growing confidently in your faith

*A lifelong journey
to becoming more like Jesus*

CAROL ROUND

Passionate
Purpose
Publishing

Grow confidently in your faith
A lifelong journey to becoming more like Jesus

Unless otherwise indicated, all scripture quotations cited in this
book are from The Holy Bible, New International Version, NIV
Copyright ©1973, 1978, 1984, 2011 by Biblica, Inc.

Any people depicted in stock imagery provided by iStockphoto
are models and such images are being used for illustrative
purposes only.

Certain stock imagery © iStockphoto.

Printed in the United States of America

Passionate Purpose Publishing
Grove, OK

For women who are searching—

searching for answers,
searching for significance,
searching for the One who can fill that emptiness.

Praise for *Growing confidently in your faith*

"Ready to spend a full year becoming more like Jesus? Read Carol Round's *Growing confidently in your faith* and you will have a biblical pattern to follow. Each month has a different focus, and every week of the month gives a new way to grow Christ-like in that attitude or action. I like how Scriptures are front and center, paired with stories and examples to help personalize each concept. Carol doesn't leave you hanging, uncertain how to grow from the book's wisdom. Each week offers ways to follow through with what you've learned. Read, apply, and before you know it, your faith will be sprouting, prepared to produce much fruit."

Kathy Carlton Willis, author and speaker, God's Grin Gal

"An inspiring and practical primer to Christian growth, *Growing confidently in your faith* is easy-to-read and enjoyable; the narrative is laced with creative anecdotes, and punctuated with pointers to gently push the reader forward into spiritual maturity."
Janey DeMeo, founder of Orphans First (www.orphansfirst.org),
Bible teacher, author of "Heaven Help Me Raise These Children!"

"In her latest devotional book, *Growing confidently in your faith: a lifelong journey to becoming more like Jesus,* columnist, author and speaker Carol Round offers women encouragement to help them grow more confident in their Christian walk. Carol, who provides a weekly column for my ASSIST News Service (www.assistnews.net), has written a must-read book for all who need encouragement, and more importantly, would like to become more like Jesus."
Dan Wooding, international author,
broadcaster and journalist

Chock-full of spiritual truth, Godly wisdom, and tips for practical application, Carol's devotional book is sure to bless its readers.

Linda W. Yezak,
author, editor, speaker

"**With great clarity and love**, in this profound devotional, Carol Round brings the principles and teachings of Jesus into our lives with practicality so we can apply them to our daily lives. With depth she shares the truths of God's Word in a manner that will pierce through doubt, shame and pain. She leaves you with a comforted heart and a real hope for the future. You will walk away each week with greater inspiration, wisdom and peace. But what draws me most to Carol's writings is her deep love for God and understanding of how He walks us through every hurt and pain, turning them to victory for His glory."

Dixie Diamanti, Life Purpose Coach,
www.reflectionsofgracehome.com

"*Growing confidently in your faith*" **will empower**, guide and inspire you to put your faith in what is true, what is good, and what is right according to God's word as you build your everlasting faith."

Valder Beebe, Host, The Valder Beebe Radio Show

"**In** *Growing confidently in your faith*," Carol Round writes as a Christian mentor to women, sharing from her personal life, from the experiences of others, and through biblical encouragement both practical and inspirational helps on how to draw closer to Jesus.

Rebecca Barlow Jordan,
inspirational author of 11 books,
including the *Day-votions*® series for women, and
a current writer for the *Mornings with Jesus* devotionals

INTRODUCTION

"When you discover who Jesus is you will discover who you are. Your identity is in Him."

Have you ever been lost? If you have, you know the uneasy feeling that comes with wandering, trying to find your way back home, trying to figure out who you are and what it is you really want and need in life.

It's like being on a journey without a map, drifting aimlessly until you reach your destination. For me, that destination was—and is—Jesus. He is my home. He is the lover of my soul. He is the One who gives my life meaning and keeps me grounded.

I was in my late 40s when I discovered how much Jesus loved me and longed to have an intimate relationship with me. My 28-year marriage had ended six weeks earlier. I was searching for meaning. My sons were grown and they didn't need me in the same way as when they were younger.

Before then, I had found my identity in being a wife, mother, daughter and high school teacher. Those roles had changed or were changing as I began filling that emptiness with material things and wrong relationships.

I had grown up in the church and been baptized at age 14. I knew of God, but I didn't have a personal relationship with Him through His Son, Jesus Christ. I had drifted away from the church, where I had found a community that kept me grounded.

On a beautiful fall afternoon in 2001, I took a break from the magazine writing assignment I was working on for a secular publication. I had writer's block and decided to seek fresh air and inspiration on a walk near the lake where I live. On my walk, I felt drawn to one of three concrete tables in a picnic area near my house. I'd never stopped on my daily walks to just sit and watch the geese making their home here. As I sat facing the water that day, I prayed aloud for the first time in my life. My prayer follows:

"Lord, I'm lost. I need your direction in my life. Please help me."

Immediately, I was filled with a peace that can only be described as having a backpack of rocks removed from my shoulders. The weight I'd been carrying was gone, replaced by joy and a lightness I can't explain. My heart beat faster and I couldn't wait to return home and finish the magazine assignment.

The article was about an 80-year-old woman who had parachuted from an airplane to celebrate that milestone birthday. Even though it was a tandem jump, I was impressed with her bravery.

When interviewing her for the story, she mentioned her pastor who thought she was too old to be taking risks. She told him, "Pastor, I could get killed crossing the street in my neighborhood. If it's my time, it's my time, but I'm going to live life to the fullest."

And she did. Her faith was grounded in her relationship with Jesus. I wrote that story over 15 years ago, but I've never forgotten her moxie. She told me, "Carol, if I lived afraid, I'd never experience what God has in store for me. I refuse to sit in a rocking chair and rust."

While I don't know if I could ever jump out of a perfectly good airplane, as I've grown in my relationship with Jesus, I've stepped out of my comfort zone more than once. I've done things I never dreamed of doing if I hadn't spent time with the Lord in prayer, Bible study and meditating on scripture.

In 2010, I traveled to Israel with a group of 45 others from my church. I walked where Jesus walked. I visited holy places and cried as I rode a boat across the Sea of Galilee. His presence was overwhelming. I also rededicated my life to Him by remembering my baptism in the Jordan River.

I've also been on numerous mission trips overseas to countries where I witnessed the poor who, in spite of their lack, were grateful for what we provided. Although there was often a language barrier, the smiles on their faces revealed they were rich in spite of their poverty.

Without a growing, abiding faith in my Savior and Lord, I would never have experienced what He has planned for my life. Looking back, I can see through His eyes how He has prepared me for my writing and speaking ministry.

I pray as you take this 52-week journey, you will grow confidently in your faith and become more like Jesus.

Hebrews 6:1 tells us, *"So let us stop going over the basic teachings about Christ again and again. Let us go on instead and become mature in our understanding (NLT).*

Are you ready to grow confidently in your faith? Let's start the journey?

TABLE OF CONTENTS

ABOUT THIS BOOK

This 52-week devotional, organized by month and theme, is designed to be used with a journal. Each Monday, you will find a devotional followed by questions for reflection. I suggest you read the devotional on Monday and scan the questions at the end. On the following days, work at your own pace, continuing to reflect on the questions and journaling your answers. You may need to reread that week's devotional before answering the questions. You can complete the questions in one sitting or spread them out over the week. The choice is yours.

I pray as you work through this devotional, you will find comfort, knowing others have been where you are. Any time during this 52-week journey, please don't hesitate to contact me at **carol@carolaround.com** if you have any questions or comments.

Also, if this book has helped on your spiritual journey, would you mind leaving a review at Amazon when you are finished? I would also be honored if you would recommend *Growing confidently in your faith* to other women.

(Note to my readers: If you write something in your journal and do not wish others to see it, them tear out that page(s) and shred them.)

January

Renew, Recommit, Rejoice

"Because of the LORD's great love we are not consumed, for his compassions never fail. They are new every morning; great is your faithfulness. I say to myself, "The LORD is my portion; therefore I will wait for him" – Lamentations 3:22-24 (NIV).

What comes to mind when you hear the words "new year?" Do positive words like new beginnings, determination and resolutions come to mind?

Or maybe you envision the hard work it will take to achieve your goals. Maybe you want to give up before you even begin.

What if I told you it's possible to begin each January full of hope without fear of disappointment and failure? What if I said you could do that every day of the year?

God's calendar doesn't begin on January 1. As Lamentations 3:22-23 tells us, *"His compassions never fail. They are new every morning."*

While January is the time when many make resolutions or set goals to get in shape, save money and get out of debt, it's also a good time for Christians to renew, recommit and rejoice. 2 Corinthians 4:16 says, *"Therefore we do not lose heart, but though our outer man is decaying, yet our inner man is being renewed day by day."*

It is my prayer that as you begin this 52-week journey you will find yourself renewed in Christ, recommitted to growing in your Christian journey and rejoicing because *"the joy of the Lord is our strength"* (Nehemiah 8:10).

WEEK 1

HOW ONE WORD CAN CHANGE YOUR LIFE

"In the beginning was the Word, and the Word was with God, and the Word was God"—John 1:1 (NIV).

If you've never made a New Year's resolution, you're in the minority. However, we all have one thing in common — time. In an article for *Pulpit Helps*, author Steven B. Cloud wrote, "As we look into a New Year, we look at a block of time. We see 12 months, 52 weeks, 365 days, 8,760 hours, 525,600 minutes, 31,536,000 seconds. And all is a gift from God."

Our lives have become so busy, yet we add to the burden each New Year by making a list of resolutions that most of us will fail to accomplish—quit smoking, lose weight and get healthy or save more money. This is just a partial list but some of the more popular ones. That's why we see so many advertisements promoting products and gyms to help us accomplish our goals. Stroll through the aisles of a bookstore and you'll find so many self-help books, it'll make you go cross-eyed with confusion.

One book, however, has the power to change your life. The Bible is filled with words of wisdom and encouragement. In Luke 11:28, Jesus says, *"Blessed rather are those who hear the word of God and obey it."*

In January 2007, Pastor Mike Ashcraft challenged his congregation to ditch their New Year's resolutions and each pick one word to focus on that year. Embracing this new idea to approaching personal change and spiritual growth, church members realized the simple plan is more effective than making an overwhelming list of resolutions each year. Why? Called God's instruction book for life, the Bible addresses every aspect of our lives—spiritually, physically, emotionally and financially.

Because we lead busy lives, we tend to focus on the surface-level of issues, forgetting God has numbered our days. Trying to manage our lives and our time, we fail miserably because we haven't taken the time to seek God's wisdom. Ultimately, says Pastor Ashcraft, that's what the "My One Word" project is all about.

Willpower and self-effort only get us so far. When we're overwhelmed with a long list, it's even more difficult to achieve lasting change. That's why, according to Ashcraft, the One-Word project works. To choose a word for the New Year, Ashcraft suggests asking the following questions:

- What kind of person do I want to become this year?

- What drives my desire to be this kind of person?

- What characteristics define this type of person? Make a list.

- Reduce your list to 10 words or less, research those words using a dictionary and Bible.

- Choose one word from your list as your word for the year.

- Choose a Bible verse that speaks to you about your chosen word and memorize it. This will provide a foundation of truth you can continually return to and will fuel your hope to change.

- What initial expectations do you have regarding the impact of your word?

One word can change your life when it is grounded in faith.

Follow Through

Renew: As you begin a new year, take the first week of January to reflect on the questions above and choose your word for this year. I have done this for several years now and I am always surprised when God leads me to select the right one for me. Some of my past words have been focus, grow and trust. I'm always surprised when the year is almost over and I realize how appropriate the chosen word was for me.

Recommit: As you begin your journey, recommit your ways to the Lord, leaving behind those things in the past holding you back from being your best for Him. Ask Him to reveal to you what you need to let go of to move forward. As Christians, we should always be moving forward.

Remember Paul's words in Philippians 3:13-14: *"Brothers and sisters, I myself don't think I've reached it, but I do this one thing: I forget about the things behind me and reach out for the things ahead of me. The goal I pursue is the prize of God's upward call in Christ Jesus"* *(CEB).*

Rejoice: After selecting your word, write it at the top of each page in your prayer journal to remind yourself of your commitment to spiritual growth.

WEEK 2

GETTING SPIRITUALLY FIT

"Forgetting what is behind and straining toward what is ahead, I press on toward the goal to win the prize for which God has called me heavenward in Jesus Christ"—Philippians 3:13-14 (NIV).

Lose weight. Get healthy. Quit smoking. Save more money. Spend more time with family. All are worthy resolutions.

When we turn the calendar to a new year, we usually reflect on where we have been and where we want to be. We look at our failures and ask ourselves, "What do I need to change?

A friend and I recently disagreed about failure. His views about failure have created eyes that see the world through cynical glasses. I believe that failure is an opportunity for growth.

You don't continue to beat a dead horse but neither do you leave him lying beside the road. Pretty soon he begins to stink.

I've heard people say, "I have no regrets about my life. If I had it to do over again, I'd do it the same way."

Not me. Although I don't wallow in the pool of regret, I'd definitely do some things differently.

We can learn from our failures to become the person God created us to be. To do that, we have to look at the past — and that requires confession. Confession is powerful. Owning up to failure is the first, painful step on the path to something better.

Changing the calendar to a new year is a good time for a spiritual checkup. When you see a new calendar, do you see days and months of blank spaces ready to be filled in with God's plans for your life or do you see a busy schedule that is taking you away from Him?

- Is your life producing something of value for God?

- Do you trust Him instead of relying on your own strength and understanding?

- Is there something in your life that is holding you back from all that God has waiting for you?

- Are you open to God's leading?

There is no magic pill that transforms us — either physically or spiritually. It requires a plan and if we fail to plan, then we plan to fail — a cliché, but true.

Becoming spiritually mature is simply a matter of learning certain spiritual exercises. Just like getting physically fit requires exercise, we must become self-disciplined in our spiritual lives. To shape our character, we must take the time to develop good habits.

Pastor Rick Warren, the author of the best-seller A *Purpose Driven Life*, says that to develop spiritual fitness, our daily habits must include time spent with God, prayer, Bible reading and obedience to what He reveals to you.

Becoming spiritually mature involves more than a quick fix. In our instant gratification society, we want it now — nuke it in the microwave for five minutes and it's done. But growing spiritually is a gradual process.

Taking the time to grow spiritually is a lifetime endeavor. Are you willing to make the commitment? It requires patience. Knowing that God isn't finished with us yet, we must press on toward the goal.

Follow Through

Renew: Have you failed in the past to stick with your New Year's resolutions? Did you examine why you failed to follow through?

Recommit: Any change we need to make in our lives requires self-discipline. Whether it's losing weight, saving money, paying off debts or kicking a bad habit, we can't accomplish our goals overnight. The same goes for spiritual fitness. Find a mentor or accountability partner to help you achieve your goals. Try working on one goal at a time instead of setting yourself up for failure by trying to do too much and becoming overwhelmed.

Rejoice: Keep track of your progress toward your goals by writing in your daily journal. Looking back at the end of each week and month will keep you motivated to move forward. Don't give up. Keep pressing on.

WEEK 3

I THINK I CAN, I THINK I CAN

"Are you so foolish? After beginning by means of the Spirit, are you now trying to finish by means of the flesh?"—Galatians 3:3(NIV).

Another year has come and gone. As we write checks to pay our bills, we have to remind ourselves that it is now a new year.

For 12 months we have written the correct year without thinking. As the days pass, we will forget the old year and our hand will automatically correct our thoughts. Wouldn't it be nice if the rest of our life was like that?

When a new year arrives, our thoughts turn to new beginnings. We set goals and vow to make changes.

Although writing a new year on our checks easily becomes a habit, it takes self-discipline to stick with our goals. Many people avoid that word: self-discipline. They claim, "I have no will power."

The will has limited power. We have to seek a power greater than ourselves to achieve long-term success with goals. Dr. Charles Stanley, pastor and president of In Touch Ministries, says a self-disciplined life must involve pleasing the Lord.

To make change a permanent part of our lives — the kind of change that improves our lives and the lives of others — we must have definite, specific goals. Writing those goals down requires us to evaluate our lives and our dreams. Goals, says Dr. Stanley, are merely statements of faith.

We can't focus on our future without setting our sights on our goals. Then, says Dr. Stanley, we have to pursue discipline with diligence.

Remember the story of *The Little Engine that Could*? The story actually has its roots in a 1906 Sunday school publication, "Wellsprings for Young People." As the story goes, a little railroad engine was asked to pull a long train of freight cars over a hill after a larger engine said, "I can't."

The little engine puffed bravely up the hill, faster and faster, as he chanted, "I think I can, I think I can, I think I can."

Sometimes we are faced with a mountain that seems insurmountable but like that little red engine, we have to focus on the ultimate goal — doing our best and being our best with the tools the Lord has given us. He may ask us to do things that seem beyond our abilities but He will always equip us for the task at hand.

When our aim is valid and we are willing to pay the price, God will grace us with the strength and direction to accomplish worthy goals. Ask yourself:

- Where do I lack self-discipline?

- Why am I having trouble reaching my goals?

- Do I have a firm sense of direction?

- Do I have a clear picture and a consuming desire to reach those goals?

- Do I have a course of action and a cooperative spirit?

- Do I have the courage to act?

- What worthy goals is the Lord asking you to accomplish today?

With a confidence in God and yourself, you can be like that little engine. I think I can, I think I can.

Follow Through

Renew: Don't beat yourself up if you have failed to accomplish your goals in the past. Remember "with God, all things are possible."

Recommit: Write a letter to God in your journal asking Him to guide you as you recommit to your goals. If you don't have a clear picture and a consuming desire to reach those goals, ask God to reveal to you what it is you need to do.

Rejoice: Listen quietly for that still, small voice after you ask for God's guidance. Peace comes when you realize God has spoken to your spirit. I've learned the following:

When peace comes, keep following His lead.

WEEK 4

LIFE IS LIKE A ROLL OF TOILET PAPER

"I press on toward the goal to win the prize for which God has called me heavenward in Christ Jesus"—Philippians 3:14(NIV).

If Mr. Whipple was still alive and doing Charmin bathroom tissue commercials, I'm sure he would agree with Andy Rooney's observation that life is like a roll of toilet paper. "The closer it gets to the end, the faster it goes."

With that statement, I would ask, "Where did last year go, and are you prepared for the New Year?" When we hear the words "new year," most of us start making resolutions to improve ourselves in the coming year. Considering that the top ten resolutions each year are similar, why do we often fail?

We start determined that this year we are going to do it. However, as the days pass and the calendar changes from January to February and then March, our determination waivers and we soon lose motivation to reach those goals.

Well-known author and speaker, Zig Ziglar, says, "People often say that motivation doesn't last. Well, neither does bathing; that's why we recommend it daily."

Starting each day by reading the Word of God is motivation for me to do what I need to do that day, even if I don't feel like it. That doesn't mean I get everything accomplished, but without encouragement from scripture and devotions, there are some days I would probably give in to despair.

I recall attending the funeral of a 28-year-old man who had died in an automobile accident. I didn't know him, but his aunt is one of my best friends. My heart ached for his family, especially for the seven-year-old son he left behind. As I listened to my friend speak about her nephew during the service, I learned that even in his short life J.J. had lived each day to the fullest.

In the book, *One Month to Live: Thirty Days to a No-Regrets Life*, authors Kerry and Chris Shook ask the question: "If you knew that you had one month to live, how would you live differently?"

What would be the focus of your days? Would your priorities change or would you continue to live life as if nothing were different?

As an experiment, the authors challenged their staff members to answer those questions by living the next 30 days as if they were their last and to write down what happened. According to the authors, the results were "nothing less than life-changing," with the group having a greater clarity of purpose and a renewed passion for the things in life that really matter.

Some people in the group did big, once-in-a-lifetime things, while others found meaning in their lives by viewing those things they once considered a chore as sacred times that could not be recaptured, like spending more time with their children or their aging parents.

What if we lived each day as if it were our last? Following in the footsteps of the apostle Paul, what if we kept pressing forward, staying focused on the Lord so we could hear those words, *"Well done thy good and faithful servant?"*

Follow Through

Renew: Starting this fourth week of the New Year, examine the goals you have set. Do they line up with God's plans for your life? Are they life-changing goals?

Recommit: Take the challenge mentioned above and live the next 30 days as if they were your last. Write down what happened.

Rejoice: When the 30 days is over, reread the things you wrote down. Has it changed your goals? Did you find your original goals as important as you thought they were?

February

Let go, Live again, Love again

"We love because he first loved us"—1 John 4:19(ESV).

What comes to mind when you hear the word "love?" Family. Happiness. Marriage. Friendship. Butterflies. Fireworks. Romance. Heartbreak. Each has a different connotation, depending on your season in life, as well as your circumstances.

If you're single, your imagination might produce visions of rose petals, Cinderella and happily-ever-after. If you've just started dating someone, romance, fireworks and butterflies might come to mind. If you're already married, your mind invokes a different picture—whether happily wed or not. Whatever your relationship status, love can take on hues of different meanings.

Have you ever thought about the different kinds of love according to God's Holy Word? The Bible explores four different types of love: divine love, brotherly love, family love and romantic love. When we discover what love really means, and how we can follow Jesus' command to "love one another," we can let go, live again and finally, love again.

In light of God's kingdom, what does this mean for you? First, if we are unable to forgive another, we really aren't living. If we want to live again, we must not only forgive others for their transgressions, we must forgive ourselves for our own mistakes. We have to let go of the past to move forward.

Matthew 6:15 says, *"But if you do not forgive others their sins, your Father will not forgive your sins."*

~13~

Many of us find it difficult to love ourselves. If we can't love who we are in Christ, how can we love another?

There's another type of love we often overlook but it's also mentioned in the Bible. In 1 Timothy 6:10, Paul writes, *"For the love of money is a root of all kinds of evil. Some people, eager for money, have wandered from the faith and pierced themselves with many griefs."*

As we explore love in this chapter, remember the great love your Abba Father has for you. John 3:16 says, *"For God so loved the world that he gave his one and only Son, that whoever believes in him shall not perish but have eternal life."*

WEEK 5

ARE YOU SUFFERING FROM STUFFITIS?

"For where your treasure is, there your heart will be also" – Matthew 6:21(NIV).

Do you suffer from "stuffitis?" What on earth is that? Is it contagious? Is it serious? Is there a cure?

First of all, let me define this disease. People who suffer from "stuffitis" are always collecting stuff. And no matter how much they collect, it is never enough. They think it is a cure for everything that ails them, especially unhappiness. They get a temporary high — a feel-good feeling — that lasts until the bills come in.

Secondly, "stuffitis" can be contagious. When we buy things to "keep up with the Joneses," then we have bought into the American lie — that more and bigger stuff will make us happy, make us the envy of the neighborhood, make us better than others.

Third, "stuffitis" is serious because it is the inability to appreciate what we have and an unending desire to have more. We go into debt with easily-obtained credit to buy more and more stuff. Then when we become bored with that stuff or think we need better stuff, we charge even more.

Eventually, this preoccupation with buying more stuff can lead to financial failure. Over 819,159 U.S. consumers filed bankruptcy in 2016.

Collecting stuff until it overruns our homes and lives is an addiction; however, it is curable. It's a painful process. But freeing yourself from this disease allows peace to enter your life and your home.

My problem is I like a bargain and when there is a sale, I head right for the racks of marked-down items. My heart races and my blood pressure rises when I see that perfect pair of shoes or a blouse that would go with my favorite skirt. It's something I have to fight because I have more than enough clothes, shoes and purses in my closet.

Armed recently with a $25 gift certificate to one of my favorite department stores, I knew what I needed when I went inside. Notice, I said needed, as in necessary, not desired.

After I used my gift certificate to purchase my necessities, I wandered to the shoe department. I was thrilled to see the winter boots, which were already half-price, marked down another 40 percent.

I tried on several pairs — six to be exact. I would have had to pay less than $25 for the pair I liked, if I had bought them. I didn't. I placed all of the boxes back on the display shelf and browsed through the racks of running shoes. I really need running shoes, not boots. But I'll wait to they go on sale.

How often do we confuse want with need? How often do we let our desires for "more, more, more" lead to a life of financial ruin?

God promises us an abundant life. An abundant life, however, is one filled with Him. If our life is filled with too much stuff, how can we make room for Him?

Does your lifestyle honor the Lord or have you become afflicted with "stuffitis?"

Follow Through

Let go: We all accumulate too much stuff. We hit sales purchasing things we don't really need. Our closets are overflowing and we often forget what we even own. I know I do. Letting go of the desire to shop is not easy. Advertisements and commercials entice us into the store where we part with our hard-earned dollars. What is the solution? Learning to live with less.

Live again: I challenge you to go through your closet and make three piles of clothing. In the first pile, place those things you really love, feel good in and have received compliments when worn. (You know what I'm talking about – that cute blouse that makes you feel good even when you're having a bad hair day.)

In the second pile, place those items you know you will never wear again because

- they don't fit or fit poorly.
- they are damaged/stained.
- they were poor decisions or hideous (though well-intentioned) gifts.
- You don't look or feel good in them.

In the third pile, place those clothes you haven't worn in a while but you're not quite ready to let go. Sometimes we hang onto things because we like them, but because our closets are so cluttered, we forget what we have.

Here's a suggestion: Try using hangers to mark off what stuff you have actually worn over time. First, turn the hangers of all your clothing away from you, and set a calendar reminder to check again in six or 12 months. After you've worn an article turn the hanger toward you. By the time you check, you'll be all to assess which ones you haven't worn. Get rid of all items you haven't worn or used.

Donate, sell or give away all items in good condition. Also, make a commitment to get rid of one item each time you purchase a new one. "Buy one, get rid of one."

Love again: What does stuff have to do with love? In Luke 12:15, Jesus says, *"Watch out! Guard yourself against all kinds of greed. After all, one's life isn't determined by one's possessions, even when someone is very wealthy."*

While there is nothing wrong with having things, did you ever stop to think how much time it takes to maintain the items we own? Whether it's our clothing, a large house or an endless array of "grown-up" toys, they require our time and attention. What if we owned less and spent more time doing the following:
- Reading and studying God's Word
- Volunteering in our church and community

- Spending more time with family, friends and neighbors in simple pleasures like conversation, picnics, outdoor games, block parties and other activities requiring less time and money

I like this quote by billionaire David Rockefeller:

"I am convinced that material things can contribute a lot to making one's life pleasant, but, basically, if you do not have very good friends and relatives who matter to you, life will be really empty and sad and material things cease to be important."

When you love your life instead of things, you will find an indescribable joy that money can't buy.

WEEK 6

THE ULTIMATE MAKEOVER

"But the Lord said to Samuel, "Do not consider his appearance or his height, for I have rejected him. The Lord does not look at the things man looks at. Man looks at the outward appearance, but the Lord looks at the heart'" — Isaiah 16:7(NIV).

Check out the cover of just about any magazine at the local supermarket and the headlines seem to taunt you:

- *Lose 25 pounds in 6 Weeks*
- *Ten Ways to Find Happiness*
- *Find the Love of your Life in 30 days*

As a society we are obsessed by perfection. We seek the perfect job, the perfect body, the perfect mate.

I remember a Reality TV show called "Extreme Makeover." The premise of the show was to take a woman who needed a complete makeover on the outside. While the results were amazing, I often wondered about the individual's inside. An extreme makeover is good for the self-esteem of those who undergo such a dramatic physical change. We all want to look our best. But looking our best and being our best are not the same.

As a child, I was shy, a bookworm. I was not athletically-inclined. In a society that values physical prowess over other personal attributes, I didn't fit. In elementary school, when teams were formed for dodge ball or some other sport, I was chosen last. Being chosen last colored my view of myself. I longed to be the most athletic, the team captain and the one who did the choosing.

I suffered from low self-esteem. Then, in my mid-forties, a friend and I started a power-walking program which eventually led to my competing in 5K races as a runner. I won a trophy for my age division in my first race.

Bitten by the racing bug, I took up the challenge of the Tulsa Run. By this time, I was no longer competing against others to win. I was competing against myself. Could I reach my personal goal to finish the race in 90 minutes?

I was encouraged by several friends who helped me pace myself during the 12-mile race. I was disappointed when, three miles from the finish line, I developed a side cramp and was forced to walk. However, through encouragement from a 75-year-old race master, I was able to sprint to the finish line.

Although I didn't win a trophy — which was not my goal — I finished in 97 minutes. It was my personal best. I knew before I started the race I would never achieve perfection by coming in first, but I knew it didn't matter. I had done my personal best.

Our relationship with God is like that race. With His encouragement, He wants us to reach the finish line. He wants us to be our personal best. He doesn't look at our outside. He doesn't see the crooked teeth or nose or other physical flaws as we do. He wants to do an extreme makeover from the inside out.

Are you ready for the most extreme makeover of your life? Look in the mirror and see the person that He does. Ask for God's guidance to change your life from the inside out. The only extreme makeover we need is finding our best selves through a personal relationship with Him

Follow Through

Let go: Ask a trusted friend — and you can return the favor if she wants — to make a list of your positive qualities.

Live again: Discuss the list with your friend and ask her to give you some ways in which she has seen you display those qualities. Ask for specific situations if she can recall them. Do likewise for her.

Love again: Post the list where you can see it on a daily basis or keep it in your Bible where you can pull it out to read when you need a pick-me-up.

Psalm 139:13-15 reminds us how much God treasures us: *"For you formed my inward parts; you knitted me together in my mother's womb. I praise you, for I am fearfully and wonderfully made. Wonderful are your works; my soul knows it very well. My frame was not hidden from you, when I was being made in secret, intricately woven in the depths of the earth"* (ESV).

WEEK 7

FORGIVENESS IS A CHOICE

"For if you forgive men when they sin against you, your heavenly Father will also forgive you" — Matthew 6:14(NIV).

As legend goes, a now-famous feud began with a dispute over the ownership of a hog. The feud escalated and lives were lost on both sides.

The battle between the Hatfields and McCoys continued for 12 years until they agreed to disagree. But it wasn't until June 14, 2003, that descendants of both sides signed a truce, though the conflict had ended a century earlier.

Lewis B. Smedes, author and professor, once said, "If we wait too long to forgive, our rage settles in and claims squatter's rights to our souls."

Four months before the last of my Dad's three brothers succumbed to cancer, I wanted my father to reconcile with him. A family dispute five years earlier had left my Dad bitter and he had refused to talk to my Uncle Joe ever since.

But my uncle was dying. I knew Dad would regret it if he did not make peace with the past. Before my uncle's death, he and my father spent many hours together talking about their childhood, among other things. They never mentioned the rift but my father was grateful for the nudge I gave him to move toward forgiveness.

Numerous scientific studies tout the benefits to our health when we forgive those who have wronged us. Chronic anger and stress are almost unavoidable consequences of an unwillingness to forgive. Both are toxic to our physical and emotional health.

Just before Christmas last year, I was led to purchase a book for a friend who was bitter about his wife's betrayal and their subsequent divorce.

As I browsed through the various books at a Christian bookstore, I asked the owner for suggestions, explaining the reason for my search. I wanted to find a book for my friend that would help him to begin the journey to freedom and eventual healing.

When she made the following statement, I asked her to write it down: "When I forgave, I set a prisoner free. Then I realized the prisoner was me."

Before I mailed the book to my friend, I wrote those words, along with the following scripture from Matthew 6;14, on the inside cover: *"For if you forgive men when they sin against you, your heavenly Father will also forgive you."*

Author Catherine Ponder once said, "When you hold resentment toward another, you are bound to that person or condition by an emotional link that is stronger than steel. Forgiveness is the only way to dissolve that link and get free."

We, as followers of Christ, are a forgiven people, but the Bible also makes it clear we are to be a forgiving people. Forgiving someone who has wronged us is not easy, but it's the only way we can be free to be the person God intends us to be.

Forgiveness is a choice and a gift we give to ourselves. It doesn't mean we forget

Follow Through

Let go: Sometimes, it's not easy to forgive someone who has wronged us. Whether it's a friend or family member, when we've been hurt, it usually leaves us angry, bitter and with a desire to seek revenge. Psychologist Sonja Lyubomirsky calls forgiveness "a shift in thinking" toward someone who has wronged you, "such that your desire to harm that person has decreased and your desire to do him good (or to benefit your relationship) has increased."

So, how can we forgive? Forgiveness is a choice. It is our decision to let go of the anger and bitterness toward the one who hurt us. Does that mean we must reconcile with that individual? Not necessarily, especially if the person is no longer living. If we haven't made peace with a family member or friend before their passing, we won't be able to move forward until we acknowledge our feelings of perceived injustice by the deceased.

In fact, it is not even necessary the other individual acknowledges our forgiveness. Forgiveness does not mean we forget, condone or excuse the other person's words or actions. However, forgiveness is a powerful choice we make to lead to greater well-being and better relationships.

Live again: Did you know forgiving someone who has hurt you is good for your health? According to the Mayo Clinic, "forgiveness brings with it plenty of health benefits, including improved relationships, decreased anxiety and stress, lower blood pressure, a lowered risk of depression, and stronger immune and heart health. Letting go of negative emotions can often have a remarkable impact on the body."

Here are some ideas to help you forgive and move forward:

- *Pray for the other person.* Also, pray for yourself, asking God to reveal how to forgive the individual who wronged you.
- *Keep a daily journal.* Pen your thoughts and emotions concerning the perceived injustice down on the lined pages. While writing, acknowledge your hurt, anger and bitterness. Journaling is a good way to help you process what happened.
- *Another way to release the pain and negative emotions is to write a letter to the individual,* whether that person is alive or deceased. In the letter, express everything you felt and are still feeling when the incident(s) occurred. Then, don't mail it or give it to the person. This process is for you to examine your feelings concerning what happened.
- *Focus on gratitude by thinking of the blessings in your life.* When we focus on the positive instead of the negative, happiness will follow from the inside out. Make a list of the blessings in your journal. Choose to do this daily.
- *Look for the lesson in the event.* Ask yourself what you might learn from it. What might you need to do in the future to prevent a similar situation? Ask yourself the following questions:

1. Do I need to develop more patience?
2. Do I need to develop more compassion for others?
3. What strengths do I need to develop?

Love again: Forgiving is a supernatural act that only Jesus Christ was capable of, but when we are hurt by someone, we hold a grudge. We want revenge and we're afraid to trust God with the situation. However, when we choose to forgive we receive a greater sense of self-worth and power.

I like this quote from Christian author and speaker Sheila Walsh: "Forgiveness is God's gift to us to live in a world that's not fair. Fair doesn't live here but Jesus does."

WEEK 8

ONLY LOVE CAN CROWD
OUT THE EVIL IN OUR WORLD

"Hatred stirs up dissension, but love covers over all wrongs" —
Proverbs 10:12 (NIV).

In a recent morning devotional, the writer shared about the loss of his
17-year-old grandson, the fatal victim of a robbery. Commenting on his
grandson, the grandfather said, "We had recently attended his high
school graduation, and he planned to enter college in the fall. He was a
handsome, loving and talented young man. Now, suddenly, he was
gone."

As the writer continued to share his story, my heart went out to him and
his family. I can't imagine the pain they've experienced. The writer
said, "The senseless murder of our grandson was not part of God's
plan. 'What,' I wondered, 'led the killers to tear a hole in the glory of
God's world?' The only answer that came to me was that evil had taken
root in their lives because love was not there to crowd it out."

As I pondered this thought, I had to agree. If someone never
experiences the love of a parent, a kind neighbor, a compassionate
school teacher, a loving church family or even the kindness of a
stranger, how do they understand the love of Christ? As the writer
above said in his devotional, "Many people who commit crimes against
their neighbors have not experienced God's love through their
interactions with others. Much of the violence in life can be prevented
if we Christians extend love to all people."

All people—even the ones whom we'd rather avoid? The ones that rub
us the wrong way or slyly insult us...do we have to love them too? Yes,
according to Jesus, even the ones who annoy us, step on our toes,
invade our personal space or whose personal habits cause us to turn up
our nose in disgust.

In Mark 12:31, Jesus tells us to *"Love your neighbor as yourself."* He didn't say "like" them. He told us to "love" them, even the least of these.

Several times a month I work at our church's food pantry, bagging groceries for those in need. Our Good Sam ministry now serves approximately 1,000 people a month. It has grown exponentially since I started serving in 2008. While it might be tempting to judge some of the "least of these," we don't know their story.

As I have become less judgmental and more loving, I have learned how far a hug and a prayer go toward helping those who seek help. And you know what? I feel loved in return.

Jesus understood two important truths we must remember: Everyone is created in God's image. Our Heavenly Father chooses to love each of His children.

Second, because we're all sinners, we're unlovable. Romans 5:8 says, *"But God demonstrates His own love for us in this: While we were still sinners, Christ died for us."*

Pastor and theologian Timothy Keller said, "If we know we are sinners saved by grace alone, we will be both open and generous to the outcasts and the unlovely."

If God can love us in our own unloveliness, surely we can love those around us.

Follow Through

Let go: Is there someone in your life, someone you avoid because he/she is unlovable? Write in your journal the reasons why this person appears unlovable to you. Reflect on his or her qualities. Does he or she have some redeeming qualities you have overlooked? What are they? Ask God to let you see this person through His eyes if you can't come up with anything positive about him/her. Look up, write down and reflect on 1 Corinthians 13:4-7.

Live again: If you are still avoiding the unlovable person, ask God to help you love that person. No person is so unlovable that he/she doesn't deserve our respect.

Love again: Everyone is created in God's image but because of sin, we're really all unlovable. However, Christ changed the rules. He offers us love, grace and forgiveness (Romans 5:8). Go out of your way this week to do something special for the unlovable in your life. You'll be surprised how it changes your view of that individual. Afterwards, journal your thoughts about the experience.

March

Prune, Plant, Produce

*"For as the soil makes the sprout come up
and a garden causes seeds to grow,
so the Sovereign Lord will make righteousness
and praise spring up before all nations"   Isaiah 61:1(NIV).*

When we think about spring, we envision seeds beginning to sprout and trees budding forth with new growth. If you love working in your flowerbeds or garden, you know it's a time to begin pruning, planting and waiting for the results of your labor.

When it comes to a healthy garden, soil preparation is important. In addition to pulling weeds, the soil must contain the correct amount and kind of nutrients for plants to produce. Just as a healthy garden requires prepping, Christians who want to produce fruit for God's kingdom must prepare their hearts and minds. How does that happen?

First, we need God's help to get rid of the weeds in our life. Weeds represent those areas in our lives that must not be allowed to "take root." For example, if we're hanging onto bitterness and unforgiveness, we must not allow them to grow unchecked.

If we want to grow spiritually and work diligently for the Lord Jesus Christ, we must read and study God's Word and let it "*dwell in us richly*" (Colossians 3:16). To mature as a Christian, we must spend time alone with Him—in meditation and prayer. God uses the spiritual disciplines of reading and meditating on His Word and praying to help us grow. Just like we fertilize and water our plants, these spiritual disciplines help us to bear more fruit.

To grow in grace is to grow in our understanding of what Jesus did for us on the cross. To grow spiritually means we appreciate the grace we have been given. The more we study God's Word and learn about Jesus, the more we will appreciate all He has done, and the more we appreciate His love and sacrifice for us, the more we will perceive the never-ending grace of God.

2 Peter 3:18 tells us to *"grow in the grace and knowledge of the Lord Jesus Christ."* Peter also affirms that we need to grow in our knowledge of Jesus so we can have an intimate relationship with Him. The more we know of Him, the more we will experience Him at work in our daily lives.

In Colossians 3:1-4, Paul writes, *"Since then, you have been raised with Christ, set your hearts on things above, where Christ is seated at the right hand of God. Set your minds on things above, not on earthly things. For you died, and your life is now hidden with Christ in God. When Christ, who is your life, appears, then you also will appear with him in glory."*

In March, we will examine the topic of allowing God to do a continual good work in us so we can bear more fruit for His kingdom.

WEEK 9

GETTING DIRTY FOR THE LORD

"He is like a well-watered plant in the sunshine, spreading its shoots over the garden"—Job 8:16(NIV)

As a child, I loved playing in the dirt, I still do. I was working in my flower beds recently doing some major overhauling when a neighbor came home from work. He hollered across the street at me, "What are you doing?"

Sitting in the dirt because my knees were hurting, I hollered back, "I'm making mud pies. Do you want one?"

Laughing, he replied, "Are you reliving your childhood?"

"Yes," I said and continued getting my hands deep into the soil. I love the feel of the cool dirt on my skin; most of the time, you won't find me wearing gardening gloves.

When other neighbors, who are out walking their dogs or taking a leisurely stroll, see me on my knees in the dirt, they often comment, "You sure are working hard."

For me, it is not work but a joy to spend that time enjoying God's wonders. You never know what you will unearth when you turn over a spade of dirt—a chubby white grub or a slimy brown fishing worm.

A friend, who had been on vacation — not away from home but from a busy time at work — recently emailed me. She had spent her days off, not on a sandy beach somewhere, but digging in the dirt and praying. She said, "It's amazing how much clutter we build up in our hearts and minds over days, weeks and even years of working and living. Digging in the dirt reminds me of how basic we really are."

Her insight made me realize why working in the soil is healing. Like most humans, we seek our creature comforts. We worry too much about what we are going to eat, how we are going to pay the bills, and how we can afford the desires of our hearts.

But when we spend time working the soil, pulling out the weeds, planting seeds and watering our plants, we are also feeding and nurturing our spiritual selves.

When I was going through some difficult times several years ago, I spent many hours in my flower beds. Although my thoughts were troubled when I first struck the dry dirt with my shovel, my heart, my mind and my spirit refused to remain in turmoil with each weed that was removed and with each flower that was tenderly rooted into the ground.

Like the flowers that grow in our gardens, we can nurture our spiritual selves or we can let the weeds of despair choke out life's joys. We have an option to mature through spiritual growth, but like the plants in our garden, we must feed and water our soul if we want to produce fruit.

Producing fruit requires time and patience. But the results are worth the effort — even if we get our hands dirty in the process.

Are you getting your hands dirty for the Lord? Feed your mind, heart and spirit. Spread your roots and bloom.

Follow Through

Prune: Is there something or someone in your life preventing you from growing spiritually? Sometimes we cling to people, places or things, thinking they are the solution to our problems. We can't move forward spiritually or emotionally until we seek God's help for the answer to what is holding us back. Grab your journal and make a list of those individuals or things of which you are afraid to let go. Examine why you are fearful of letting go.

Plant: Ask God to help you let go of those things hindering you from a better future. Write a letter to Him in your journal seeking His guidance. Ask Him the following questions:

1. Abba Father, I know I need to let go of _____ (a thing or a person's name) and move on. Please show me how to let go. Stop and *listen* for that still small voice. If you are sincere in your desire to leave the past behind, God will respond if you are open.

2. Father, Your Word says, *"For I know the plans I have for you, says the Lord. They are plans for good and not for evil, to give you a future and a hope."* Father, help me to understand your plans one step at a time.

3. Father, I want to grow spiritually. Open my eyes, my heart and my spirit to reveal Your Son to me as I meditate on Your Word.

Produce: Continue to seek your Heavenly Father each morning in reading scripture, praying and writing in your prayer journal. Make it a daily habit! Spending time with Your Creator is a spiritual discipline to help you grow more like Jesus.

WEEK 10

WELCOME TO THE CROWD

"The apostles said to the Lord, 'Increase our faith!'"— Luke *17:5(NIV).*

"I have faith. I just want proof to back it up." Those words, spoken by an actor in a movie I watched recently, reminded me that many of us struggle sometimes to have faith.

Unexpected expenses cause bills to pile up on our desk. A loved one is diagnosed with an incurable disease. A job loss leaves a father wondering how he will support his family.

Life experiences can cause our faith to expand and deflate like a hot air balloon. Have you felt that way? I know I have.

Have you felt at times that your faith is shrinking instead of growing? Welcome to the crowd. Even Jesus' disciples knew they needed more faith. They begged Him, "Increase our faith!"

When I read this passage, I realized that even those who were closest to Jesus didn't exhibit super faith or impeccable behavior. However, they knew what they needed, and they asked.

A friend, who has overcome many life disappointments, shared an encouragement which she hands to friends and strangers, along with a small rock. On the blue card is the following inspiration from Mark 11:22-23: *"Have faith in God," Jesus answered. "I tell you the truth, if anyone says to this mountain, 'Go throw yourself into the sea,' and does not doubt in his heart, but believes that what he says will happen, it will be done for him."*

Instructions on the card read: **Please follow directions as needed to conquer your mountain! When you feel defeated, put your rock on the floor in front of you. Stand on it. Now you have conquered it.**

If it stands in your way, with your rock on the floor, walk around it. There is always another way.

If it bothers you, kick your rock to the side. Then cast it away, because you will not walk in offense. Now pick it up. You have done the impossible. You have moved a mountain.

This is your mountain. God said to move it. You just thought it was bigger. This rock was once a boulder. This boulder was once a mountain. Remember, mountains are only as large as you see them.

Some people read Mark 11:22-23 and become frustrated because they have faith and the mountains don't seem to be moving. We can believe and we can try but sometimes that mountain won't budge.

Recently, when I wanted to build a new flowerbed, I had to move rocks. Some were part of my plan; others were not. Sometimes the rocks were heavy and could only be moved one at a time. I felt frustrated because I seemed to be making little progress. Hours later, I stood back amazed. The mountains had been moved.

Faith still moves mountains but sometimes the greater act of faith is not seeing the mountain move instantly. We have to work with God to move it bit by bit.

What is the mountain in your life? Just ask God for more faith and watch that mountain become a pile of rocks.

Follow Through

Prune: Faith still moves mountains but sometimes we need help to remove the barriers from our lives—barriers blocking our unbelief. Grab your journal and start listing the things that come to mind when your faith is lagging. Then, locate scripture that addresses your mountain, i.e. finances, illness, etc. Write those scriptures down. Memorize them. Proverbs 6:21-22 reads, *"Bind them on your heart always; tie them around your neck. When you walk, they will lead you; when you lie down, they will watch over you; and when you awake, they will talk with you"* (ESV).

Plant: What are your mountains? If you're facing an insurmountable pile of debts, maybe you need to consult an agency with experience in debt relief. Does your church provide assistance? If your church doesn't offer a course, maybe you can find someone in your church to lead Dave Ramsey's Financial Peace University class. Better yet, you can volunteer because the course comes with a DVD as well as all the necessary materials to go through the nine-week class to eventual financial freedom. You don't have to be debt free yourself to lead this class.

If your mountain involves a serious illness, seek support from your church family. Ask for prayer or whatever else you need as you're going through this unexpected health crisis. Journal your emotions and ask God for healing, comfort and peace. Isaiah 41:10 says, *"Fear not, for I am with you; be not dismayed, for I am your God; I will strengthen you, I will help you, I will uphold you with my righteous right hand" (ESV).*

Produce: As the mountain barring your way begins to come down, ask God to "increase your faith." Thank Him for chipping away at the mountain standing before you and trust Him to continue to do so. Ask Him what your part is in removing the mountain.

WEEK 11

MAKER OF ALL THINGS, INCLUDING MUD

*"Through him all things were made; without him
nothing was made that has been made" — John 1:3 (NIV).*

"In the beginning, God created the heavens and the earth." Even for
those who are not Bible scholars, the first verse in the first chapter of
the Old Testament is familiar.

God also created mud. As I was walking at a local park on a recent
warm spring day, I saw two children playing by the lake. My first
reaction when I saw what they were doing was, "Oh, my gosh! I'd hate
to wash their clothes." The boy and girl, around nine-years-old, were
having a mud fight.

My second reaction, when I saw their joy was, "That looks like fun."
That insight came from knowing the Lord and experiencing His
creations, even mud.

As a child, I also enjoyed God's creations. My sister and I loved
making mud pies after a spring rainfall. When we were finished, our
mother usually hosed us down outside before we were allowed in the
house.

As an adult, I am saddened when I see the thoughtlessness of people
who carelessly throw their trash along the roadside and in other public
places. Although God gave humankind the capability of inventing new
products, like plastic and aluminum, they often end up on the ground
where they are a threat to the wildlife and the environment.

I was amazed, yet troubled, by a fact sheet I received with one of my
utility bills. In the informative pamphlet, I learned the following about
the litter that dots our landscape and threatens to destroy God's
beautiful creation. It takes 10-20 years for plastic bags to biodegrade
while aluminum cans last as long as 100 years.

Other statistics were even more disheartening. Here are a list of products scattered about as litter and the years required for disintegration:

- Styrofoam cups, 1-100 years
- tin cans, 50-100 years
- plastic 6-pack holder rings, 450 years
- glass bottles, one million years
- plastic bottles, forever

These statistics are astounding, even more so in light of our world's wastefulness.

A previous neighborhood in which I lived had an overabundance of foot traffic because people cut through on their way to a local store. It was frustrating for me because careless shoppers' trash littered the streets and yards. I started taking a sack with me to retrieve the waste on my daily walks.

Scripture teaches that the earth belongs to God. *"The earth is the Lord's, and everything in it, the world, and all who live in it..."* (Psalm 24:1). It is not ours to do with as we please.

In Genesis 2:15, one of God's first commandments to Adam says we are to "take care of" creation.

Humankind, however, has not listened very well to the Maker of Heaven and Earth. We have an obligation to protect and restore the gift of God's beloved creation; however, we have to take action to better honor Him and show that we are good stewards of all that He has given us.

Life is God's gift to you. The way you live it is your gift to God. How are you living your life?

Follow Through

Prune: Examine your daily habits. How do you dispose of your trash? Can it be recycled? Find out where the closest recycling center is to you and begin a recycling newspapers, aluminum cans, plastic bottles, etc.

Plant: Start a neighborhood recycling program or one at your church. If you have children or grandchildren, teach them about taking care of God's creation. Involve them in a recycling program.

Produce: If you're a crafty person, look for ways to recycle your own trash into repurposed items. If you google, "repurposed items," you'll find a plethora of DIY websites. You just might find a new source of revenue for your bank account if you can sell your repurposed products.

WEEK 12

IS YOUR TONGUE "HOLEY?"

"Set a guard over my mouth, O Lord; keep watch over the door of my lips"— Psalm 141:3 (NIV).

A friend and I were recently discussing the different times in our lives when we wished we had just kept our mouths shut. We've all been there, saying the wrong thing at the wrong moment. Some of us have even earned a t-shirt for "foot-in-mouth" disease.

After we had a lively talk about some of these embarrassing and hurtful moments, my friend told me about a pastor's wife she knew who had trouble keeping her mouth shut. I found the story amusing because the wife revealed she had "a holey tongue."

My friend explained that since this woman knew she had trouble holding her tongue or refraining from speaking her mind, she had resorted to biting it to keep from saying things she should not. Therefore, she had come up with the expression, "holey tongue."

I like this woman's attitude because I have had to learn, the hard way, to keep my mouth shut when I thought I had all of the answers. Like David, I have to ask God continually to keep a guard over my mouth.

Author Robert Newton Peck once said, "Never miss a chance to keep your mouth shut."

Following that advice is not always easy, especially when someone has made an unkind remark or passed judgment. It takes self-control and learning to use the opportunity to grow within yourself when you would rather strike back. I haven't always been successful either.

Psalm 52:4 describes the tongue as a "sharpened razor." If you have ever been cut with a sharp razor or knife, you know the results. If the cut is deep enough, you bleed. The same thing happens when your words hurt someone's feelings. Once you say something, you can't take it back. You can apologize and ask for forgiveness, but the words still hang in the air and color the relationship.

I remember the old rhyme, "Sticks and stones will break my bones but words will never hurt me." I can also recall shouting those words when I was a child and involved with others in a neighborhood spat. The truth is words do hurt, not physically, but emotionally.

In Proverbs 12:18, wise King Solomon wrote, *"Reckless words pierce like a sword, but the tongue of the wise brings healing."*

I am glad that God's mercies are new each morning because I have been reckless with my words in the past. I don't want to be remembered for those times when my tongue got the best of me. Instead, I want my words to be ones that encourage and lift people up.

As followers of Christ, we are a work-in-progress. He is not finished with us yet. Therefore, I will keep trying with His help to harness my tongue and follow James' advice in 1:19 *"to be quick to listen, slow to speak and slow to anger."*

I also plan to follow the advice of the pastor's wife and develop a "holey" tongue.

Follow Through

Prune: Recall times when you've spoken out and hurt another, embarrassed yourself or another or said things you wish you could stuff back into your mouth. We've all done it. No one is immune from "foot-in-mouth" disease. Do any of the times you can recall still haunt you today? Grab your journal and write about any of those incidents that are still bothering you. Ask yourself how you could have better handled the situation.

Plant: In James 3:5, the writer points out that *"the tongue is a little member that boasts great things."* In verse 8, James adds, *"The tongue can no man tame; it is an unruly evil, full of deadly poison."* We are reminded in these verses of the power of the tongue. How can we tame it? With God's help we can. Here are some suggestions adapted from the book, *Keep it Shut* by Karen Ehman:

1. **Choose Grace:** Each day we have options, options to be frustrated, hurt, irritated, angry or judgmental about what someone else has done. Maybe a family member left a mess in the kitchen or one of your children broke a favorite vase. Maybe your husband forgot your anniversary or your best friend forgot your birthday. Maybe someone cut you off in traffic or cut in front of you in the grocery store line while you were perusing the magazines at the checkout.

    As humans, we default to our emotions, feeling disappointed, angry, judgmental or frustrated. We experience a myriad of negative emotions. In all of these situations, we do have a choice—to choose grace. Even when we don't want to—"They hurt me." Even when they don't really deserve it—"It was their fault."

    But grace is offered, even when the offender doesn't deserve it. Because that is exactly what grace is—undeserved.

2. **Listen More Than You Speak:** Remember, you have two ears and one mouth. Be sure to listen as much as you speak. Ehman's admits her family sometimes calls her the "Gap Filler," because she's the one always eager and willing to fill any gap or pause. She says, "I tend to get nervous in new social situations and my nervousness can result in being extra chatty.

    We can avoid misunderstandings by talking less and listening more, she adds. "It is easy to jump to the wrong conclusion, especially when we haven't had a chance to hear all the facts. While you might often regret speaking too soon, you will never regret taking the time to really listen."

3. **Say Nothing:** Remember the old proverb: *If you can't say something nice, don't say it at all.* Don't offer insincere flattery. It can get us in almost as much trouble as criticism. Silence really is golden. No one can fault you for words you haven't said. To keep from blurting out things you might later regret, try counting to10, 20 or, if necessary, to 100, before speaking. You may even need to literally bite your tongue to keep it under control.

4. **Examine Your Motives**: Before speaking, ask yourself, "Why do I feel led to say this?" Is it jealousy? Insecurity? Retaliation? Seriously examine your motives before opening your mouth. Being in tune with your motives can save you embarrassment.

5. **Watch Your Words**: Before you speak, ask yourself, Are "the words I am about to speak the ones I really want others to remember me for? Are my words encouraging, constructive, truthful and kind? Do my words build someone up, rather than tearing them down? Are my words factual and wise? Do I listen to the other person before I speak? If not, consider rephrasing your words or not speaking at all.

Produce: As you follow the advice above, note in your journal how it is helping you to tame your tongue. Give God praise for His help.

WEEK 13

ARE YOU A WORRYWART?

"Therefore do not worry about tomorrow, for tomorrow will worry about itself. Each day has enough trouble of its own" — Matthew 6:34(NIV).

"If worry were an effective weight-loss program, women would be invisible." When I read this quote recently, I had to laugh because it's the truth. Does that mean women worry more than men do?

Regardless of your gender, almost everyone worries about something whether it is finances, health, work, or family issues. However, if you worry 24/7, you just might be a worrywart.

According to dictionary.com, a worrywart is defined "as a person who tends to worry habitually and often needlessly." Recent studies indicate that 85 percent of all that we worry about never happens. These include worries over our past, which we can never change, worries over which we have no control, irrational concerns or fears and future worries.

Over 100 diseases have been directly attributed to worry. The strength of your immune system is related to many factors, including worry. Worry not only robs you of your physical energy, it can steal your peace of mind. Worry can raise your blood pressure, harden your arteries, and put wrinkles on your face and dark circles under your eyes.

Worry will not make your problems go away, help you deal with your problems, or make you feel better. It only robs you of today's joy.

We can easily become discouraged by daily headlines of doom and gloom. But can we change those things? I like this anonymous quote: "Worry is like a rocking chair; it keeps you busy, but it doesn't get you anywhere."

So what is the answer to worry? If you believe scripture, then the only answer is prayer. When we are facing difficulties, we should focus on God and not the problem because He has our best interests at heart.

We should also focus on His resources and what He has promised us in scripture; third, we should not focus on the obstruction but look at it as an opportunity for God to demonstrate His love.

I recall reading a devotional titled "God's Bag." The writer instructed readers to write their worries down and place them in a brown paper bag. Following the instructions was this letter:

My dear child,
Today I will be handling all your problems. Please remember that I do not need your help. Write your worries down and kindly place them in the God bag. It will be addressed in my time, not yours. Once the matter is placed into the bag, do NOT hold on to it or remove it. Holding on will delay the resolution of your problem. If it is a situation you think you can handle, please consult me in prayer first. Because I do not sleep, there is no need for you to lose sleep. Rest my child. If you need to contact me, I am only a prayer away.

Love,
Your Heavenly Father

Because the Lord our God is with us always, we need not worry about tomorrow.

Follow Through

Prune: What do you worry about? While there are many things to cause us stress each day, we must remember God is in control. Most of what we worry about never comes to pass. Grab your journal and tell God what is bothering you. Ask Him to bring you peace about the situation and trust that He will.

Plant: Start a "worry" bag or even a "worry" jar. Each time you worry about something, write it down and place it in the container you chose. Give it to God.

Produce: At the end of each month, go back through your "worry" container. Note in your journal those things you worried about that never happened. Note anything in your journal you still worry about and ask God to help you let it go.

April

Acknowledge, Accept, Anticipate

"Acknowledge and take to heart this day that the Lord is God in heaven above and on the earth below. There is no other" —
Deuteronomy 4:39(NIV).

What if someone asked you the following question: "Why do you follow Jesus?" An atheist posed that question to me on social media one day.

Since I was only allowed 124 characters to reply, I said, "I never understood who I really was, my identity, until I realized how much He loved me. He loved me enough to die for me."

Many Christians don't understand Jesus wants a personal relationship with each of us. I was in my late 40s before I understood. Attending church each Sunday doesn't make us a Christian. We can accept Jesus as our Savior but until we make Him the Lord of our lives, we'll never fully grasp the meaning of His sacrifice for us.

Before I acknowledged Jesus as my Lord, my identity was defined by my roles in life: daughter, wife, mother and teacher. If someone had asked me to identify who I was, I could have told them my name; however, does a name given to us at birth define who we are in Christ? Once I accepted the best identity a woman can embrace — a daughter of the most high God — I eagerly began to anticipate a growing relationship with Him and what that meant for my future, a future filled with adventure as I began to trust Him on my new journey.

In April, we will look at the different facets of drawing closer to and understanding how a personal relationship with Christ transforms us from the inside out.

WEEK 14

AND THAT HAS MADE
ALL THE DIFFERENCE

"Here I am! I stand at the door and knock. If anyone hears my voice and opens the door, I will come in and eat with him, and he with me"
— Revelation 3:20 (NIV).

I grew up attending a small church only a block from where my sister and I grew up. We walked to Sunday school each week with other neighborhood children. I attended faithfully until I married at age 19— really too young to understand what that lifelong commitment entailed.

Eventually I drifted away from the church. And though I have always believed in God, I didn't know Him.

We can attend church every time the doors are open. We can listen to the sermon, sing hymns of praise, participate in church activities and still walk out the door without knowing the Lord personally.

In late 2001—after my 28-year marriage ended— I realized something was missing in my life. I didn't know what it was. I felt a gnawing emptiness inside that nothing could ease.

Shopping for clothes, shoes, purses and jewelry gave me a temporary high. Staying busy to occupy every waking moment didn't fill that hole. Escaping through reading one fiction book after another provided no relief. Working harder to earn more money couldn't fill me up. Neither could the various dating relationships I had.

Nothing could fill that void in my heart except a personal relationship with my Savior. He continued to patiently knock at the door of my heart until I opened it and invited Him in. And that has made all the difference.

God's patience with me has helped me to be more patient with those around me. His acceptance of me—faults and all—has made me less critical of others. His willingness to forgive me has led me to forgive those who have hurt me. By His grace, I am a new person.

I sometimes refer to myself as the "old Carol" and the "new Carol" when talking about the changes Christ has made in me. Those who know me best have seen the transformation.

Another word for transformation is adaptation. The definition of adaptation, according to dictionary.com, "is the acquisition of modifications in an organism that enable it to adjust to life in a new environment."

I have willingly allowed the Lord to transform me so that I can adjust to life in a new environment—an environment of love and acceptance because He first loved and accepted the person I was and who I have become through a personal relationship with Him.

I am still working, with His help, on becoming the woman He created me to be. I am a work-in-progress like the pieces of a puzzle that must patiently be fitted together to form the whole picture.

Many people have the pre-conceived idea that when you accept the Lord into your life, all of your troubles will magically disappear. Actually, my disappointments, my heartaches and serious illnesses have increased—but then so has my faith.

When I began to feel unfulfilled and empty, I think Jesus was knocking louder. His knock was more urgent, louder. He was preparing me for what was to come. I'm so thankful He kept knocking, so blessed He didn't give up on me.

Is He knocking at your door? Why not open it and let Him in?

Follow Through

Acknowledge: If you're a believer and have accepted Jesus as your Savior, have you made Him the Lord of your life? What does it mean to you to make Jesus the Lord of your life?

First, it's a lifelong process of submitting your will to Him every day. It begins with your willingness to develop a relationship with Him.

How do we develop that relationship? Just like we do in any other relationship: by spending time with Him through reading God's Holy Word, prayer and meditation and periods of solitude.

Accept: When we accept what the scripture commands believers to do, we go one step further in cementing a deeper relationship with Jesus. For example, John 15:17 commands believers to love one another. Obeying God's commands is part of the process to growing spiritually. Which, of any, of God's commands is a struggle for you? Pray and journal, asking God to reveal the answer.

Anticipate: When we began pursuing a personal relationship with Jesus, the choices we make will honor Him. Do we always get it right? No, but that's what grace is all about. Each time you make a decision to obey God's commands, keep moving forward to the next step. Be sure and document those milestones in your journal.

WEEK 15

PUTTING ONE FOOT
IN FRONT OF THE OTHER

"When you walk, your steps will not be hampered; when you run, you will not stumble" — Proverbs 4:12 (NIV).

In my mid-40s, the racing bug hit me after I began an exercise routine to lose weight. A friend and I became walking partners, and on a lark, we entered our first 5K race. We had planned to power walk the 3.1 miles for fun. We weren't trying to win a medal or trophy.

However, about a mile into the race, I was inspired — or should I say challenged — by some of my high school students to run. More competitive than I realized, I couldn't let their "taunts" get the best of me. I finished third in my age division but not without paying the price.

In addition to a trophy, I also earned shin splints because I was not wearing the proper footwear. Running shoes and walking shoes are designed differently.

Before entering the next competition, I did my research and purchased the correct shoes for running. It made a difference in the outcome. I earned a second place medal in the next race and was able to walk without pain afterwards.

Wouldn't it be nice if we could say the same about this journey called life? That it was as easy as making the right purchase to eliminate the pain. However, it's not that simple.

Each of us has to make choices. Because we are uniquely endowed by our Creator with different strengths, our life paths are different. Sometimes we find ourselves at a crossroads in life, not certain which path to take. Fear of the unknown can stop us before we get to the finish line.

Think about Abraham who was called by God to leave his family. He left everything familiar to set out on a new journey in life. He had to make a choice to take that next step. Abraham left his comfort zone after placing his trust in God. He didn't have a detailed blueprint from God, revealing each leg of this new adventure, but he took that next step.

Christian author C.S. Lewis once said, "What saves a man is to take a step. Then another step."

Observe a young child who is just learning how to walk. He will cling to his parents' hands or a nearby object before he finally gains the courage to let go. Of course, he will fall many times before he is able to take several steps on his own. It's part of the process of letting go and taking the next step.

Sometimes, it requires more than a baby step. It takes a giant leap of faith as small as a mustard seed. Mustard seeds are tiny, about three millimeters in diameter. If you converted that into inches, it would equate to 0.1181. Can you find that on your ruler?

God doesn't ask us to stop and measure the distance, but He does require us to take the next step. With faith and courage, we can put one foot in front of the other.

Are you ready to take the next step of faith?

Follow Through

Acknowledge: Look up a photo of a mustard seed on the Internet. Remember what Jesus said in Matthew 17:20? *"For I assure you: If you have faith the size of a mustard seed, you will tell this mountain, 'Move from here to there,' and it will move. Nothing will be impossible for you'" (HCSB).*

We don't need a mountain of faith to take the next step, just the faith the size of a mustard seed.

Accept: Accept that God has a greater plan for your life than you can ever imagine. What step of faith is he asking you to take today? Begin a journal entry with the following and then listen for that still small voice leading you to take the next step of faith:

Dear Abba Father,
I am ready for the next step in my walk with you. What would you have me do?

Get quiet and listen for that still, small voice. Surrender your will to His. *"Not my will but yours be done."*

Anticipate: When God opens the door, don't hesitate but willingly move forward into the future He has for you. While we don't know what the next step will be in our walk, we can eagerly and patiently wait for His guidance.

A prayer for while you wait:

Lord, help me to embrace Your plan, even when the circumstances in my life are not what I desire. Allow me to see that You are working for my good. I know that nothing takes You by surprise. Please help me to embrace Your future for my life through obedience, trust and seeking You. In Jesus' name, I pray. Amen.

WEEK 16

ARE YOU LIVING LIFE BACKWARDS?

"You show that you are a letter from Christ, the result of our ministry, written not with ink but with the Spirit of the living God, not on tablets of stone but on tablets of human hearts" — 2 Corinthians 3:3 (NIV).

For many years, I lived life backwards. Motivated by envy, I wanted what others had and I didn't. Caught up in what the world said I needed to be happy, I was lost until I came to understand the truth of what God has to offer His children.

Because I have been there, I can relate when someone expresses unhappiness with his or her life. However, I have learned that when you are willing to do what God asks, you will experience a life of fulfillment that money cannot buy. I didn't learn this lesson overnight or by osmosis. I had to live it.

I like this quote by Margaret Young, a popular singer and comedienne in the United States in the 1920s: "Often people attempt to live their lives backwards; they try to have more things or more money, in order to do more of what they want, so they will be happier. The way it actually works is the reverse. You must first be who you really are, then do what you need to do, in order to have what you want."

The first step for me was discovering who I am in Christ. When I defined myself by other people's expectations, I had no clue who I really was. Therefore, I spent much of my life pleasing others and what I thought I wanted in life did not line up with God's Word.

When I look back at where I was and where I am now, I am truly amazed at God's goodness. While I have been a wordsmith since I was old enough to pick up a pen, I never envisioned I would be using my gift to glorify Him. But when I trusted God, He began to help me live life forward and to live it for Him.

Religious leader, Henry B. Eyring, once said, "Love is the motivating principle by which the Lord leads us along the way towards becoming like Him, our perfect example. Our way of life, hour by hour, must be filled with the love of God and love for others."

I have a friend named Sharon who loves to share her testimony of living in a fog for too many years. Her history includes childhood abuse and an alcoholic husband. Once she embraced her past, God turned her mess into a message.

During an afterschool church program one day, Sharon had decorated the classroom for Valentine's Day. Excited, the children asked why she had done so much for them. She replied, "It's a ministry for me."

She asked the youngsters if they knew the definition of ministry.

One wise seven-year-old responded, "It's like a little door opens in your heart and lets you know that you love someone and you want to serve them."

I think this youngster has it figured out. Don't you?

Follow Through

Acknowledge: Reread Margaret Young's quote on the previous page and ask yourself if you've been living life backwards? Journal your response to this epiphany.

Accept: Do you know who you are in Christ? Do you live to please others or Him? If you're uncertain, take time to reflect on your life and the decisions you've made. Were those decisions based on a life lived for Jesus or for your own happiness? Writing in your prayer journal can help you find those answers.

Anticipate: Once you accept your new identity in Christ and live for Him — serving and loving others — you will find your happiness multiplied into joy. What are your thoughts on the difference between happiness and joy? Look up the definitions. Do they agree with your thoughts?

WEEK 17

HAVE YOU FOUND YOUR PURPOSE?

"It's in Christ that we find out who we are and what we are living for. Long before we first heard of Christ and got our hopes up, He had his eye on us, had designs on us for glorious living, part of the overall purpose He is working out in everything and everyone"— Ephesians *1:11-12 (MSG).*

A website I came across one day proclaimed the following: "How to Finally Find Your Purpose!" Curious, I checked out the claim.

According to the authors, "If you feel stuck, unhappy or overwhelmed in your career or life, we know just what you need." They also offered ways to get unstuck, including an eight-step life plan. I liked some of the suggestions.

However, after reading much of the website, I realized one important factor was missing — God's plans. Like many self-help authors, these writers overlooked one of the most important aspects of our lives — learning the reason for your being.

Did you know you were born with a God-given purpose? If you didn't know that, you are not alone.

Minister Gillis Triplett offers these six Bible verses to affirm our reason for being:
- Every human being entered into the earth realm with a God-given purpose *(Ecclesiastes 3:1).*
- No man or woman ever born came without a God-given purpose (*II Timothy 1:9*).
- Everyone was born with gifts, talents and abilities to assist them in fulfilling their God-given purpose (*Romans 11:29*).
- It is the responsibility of each individual to learn his or her God-given purpose (*Romans 12:2*).
- You must be able to convey your God-given purpose to others (*Habakkuk 2:2*).

If you fail or refuse to seek out your God-given purpose, your options automatically become:

- your own personal vision for your life
- society's vision for your life, or
- the devil's vision for your life.

With these plans, you may experience great financial success, but in the end, none of these visions will bring you fulfillment, satisfaction or peace of mind (*Proverbs 19:21*).

When I taught high school, I observed that some students chose careers based on potential earnings in a field. However, many dropped out of college or changed their majors more than once because they did not understand that, prior to birth, God placed in each one of us the necessary gifts, talents and abilities we would need to fulfill His purpose for our life.

Playwright George Bernard Shaw wrote:

"This is the true joy in life, the being used for a purpose recognized by yourself as a mighty one; the being thoroughly worn out before you are thrown on the scrap heap; the being a force of nature instead of a feverish selfish little clod of ailments and grievances complaining that the world will not devote itself to making you happy."

Humorist and author, Erma Bombeck, said, "When I stand before God at the end of my life, I would hope that I would not have a single bit of talent left, and could say, 'I used everything you gave me.'"

I hope I will be able to say the same. Will you?

Follow Through

Acknowledge: Have you discovered your purpose in life? What is it? How did you arrive at this discovery?

Accept: If you haven't discovered why you are here, take time to journal, reflect and ask God to help you use your gifts and talents for His glory.

Anticipate: Reread and think about the two quotes on the previous page from George Bernard Shaw and Erma Bombeck. What do these statements mean to you as a follower of Christ? Do you think an unbeliever would understand their statements? Why or why not?

May

Communicate, Cherish, Celebrate

"Start children off on the way they should go, and even when they are old they will not turn from it"—Proverbs 22:6 (NIV).

While men father children, women who become mothers are connected to their children in a way no one else can fathom. If you've ever given birth, you understand.

As mothers, we relish every milestone in the lives of our children — the first step, the first word, the first day of school and each "first" they experience before growing up and leaving home.

What words come to mind when you think of the word "mother"? When we're young, our mother is our nurturer, a disciplinarian, a nurse and our first teacher. She's selfless and loving, sacrificing many of her own wants and needs for her children. Mothers want to make sure their children are equipped with the knowledge, skills and abilities they need to become competent human beings and adults.

Being a mother is not easy but it's the most rewarding job a woman will ever experience. I like this quote by Pastor Charles Stanley:

> "Motherhood is a great honor and privilege, yet it is also synonymous with servanthood. Every day women are called upon to selflessly meet the needs of their families. Whether they are awake at night nursing a baby, spending their time and money on less-than-grateful teenagers, or preparing meals, moms continuously put others before themselves."

In May, we'll look at mothers and their roles.

WEEK 18

THROW AWAY YOUR GUILT KIT

"All the prophets testify about him that everyone who believes in him receives forgiveness of sins through his name" — Acts 10:43 (NIV).

If you're a mom, or can remember your mother doing the following, then you can appreciate these words I read on a coffee mug recently: "Mom, I'll always love you but I'll never forgive you for cleaning my face with spit on a hanky!"

I had to laugh aloud because I have been on both ends, the receiving and the giving. However, I didn't use a hanky. I used my hand and I can still remember my sons ducking when they saw me wetting my fingertips to wipe their face or slick down a wild cowlick.

Mothers probably carry around more guilt than most. When our teenagers or adult children make poor choices, we start examining what we did wrong as a parent. As a mother who carried and nourished the new life for nine months in her body, the connection is even stronger. I think that might be the reason we tend to accept their failures as our failures. They were literally connected to us through the umbilical cord that provided everything necessary for their growth and survival.

Most of us can relate to feelings of guilt at one time or another in our lives. In addition, some of us find it hard to forgive ourselves for the bad choices we have made.

I was amazed by the following story as told by Steve Goodier:

"I read of a New Jersey artist who capitalized on people's need to let go of the past by selling them 'guilt kits.' Each kit contained 10 disposable brown paper bags and a set of instructions which said, 'Place bag securely over your mouth, take a deep breath and blow the guilt out. Dispose of bag immediately.' Amazingly, 2,500 kits sold at $2.50 each. But perhaps not so amazing when you think of the guilt many of us carry around."

In "The Capitol of the World," a short story by Ernest Hemingway, a Spanish father seeking reconciliation with his son, places a newspaper ad that reads, "Paco, meet me at Hotel Montana noon Tuesday. All is forgiven." When the father arrives, he is astounded to find 800 young men named Paco waiting for their fathers.

While we can never underestimate the need for forgiveness and restoration to wholeness, I have learned the true path to letting go of guilt and seeking forgiveness must begin with accepting Christ as your Savior.

In Lee Strobel's *The Case for Easter*, the investigative journalist writes about his search to find evidence for the resurrection. When Strobel, a former atheist, sets out to distinguish fact from myth, he didn't know he would eventually find the real truth. At the end of his journey, he said, "Because of the evidence, I now believed Jesus to be the Son of God. But to become his child, it was necessary for me to receive the free gift of forgiveness that he purchased with his life on the cross."

You don't need to buy a guilt kit. All it requires from you is a simple "yes" to Jesus. Accept His eternal gift.

Follow Through

Communicate: If you're a mother, do you carry around any guilt feelings connected to raising your children — whether they are still at home or grown? If so, express in your journal why you feel that way.

Cherish: Realize we all make mistakes. None of us is immune. Remember and cherish those things you know you did right as a mother. Make a list in your journal and give thanks to God for your children.

Celebrate: Reread and think about the two stories in the devotional above. Why do you think so many of us carry around guilt about our mistakes? Is it hard to forgive yourself for your mistakes? Why or why not? Celebrate Jesus' sacrifice on the cross. He died to release us from our sins and free us from guilt.

WEEK 19

WHAT'S THE BEST ADVICE?

"Listen to advice and accept instruction, and in the end you will be wise" — Proverbs 19:20 (NIV).

"You'll shoot your eye out." If you've ever watched the classic movie "A Christmas Story," you might be able to relate to Ralphie who was trying to convince his parents to buy him a Red Ryder BB gun as a gift. In the 1940s, the Red Ryder was a popular boy toy.

We can all remember similar advice from our parents like "wash behind your ears," "do unto others," "bundle up or you'll catch a cold," and the list could go on. Our elders love giving advice. However, it doesn't stop there. We're bombarded daily with advice on talk shows, like Dr. Phil and Oprah, to the evening news bytes, giving us health warnings. Those warnings aren't necessarily bad either.

When was the last time you found yourself offering what you considered helpful advice to someone else but he or she did not take it that way? If you care about others and hate to see them troubled, it's hard to refrain from giving what we feel is "friendly" advice.

If you're a parent, you're probably also prone to giving advice, especially when you see your grown children making mistakes. I can still recall advice I received from my parents when they were still alive.

Now, I can look back at the poor choices I made and the advice I didn't heed because I thought I knew better. I've come to the conclusion that those who are older are, for the most part, wiser. They've lived what younger people are experiencing.

Ecclesiastes 1:9 says, *"What has been will be again, what has been done will be done again; there is nothing new under the sun."*

Although we live in a rapidly changing world often defined by the latest technology gadget, people have not changed. Study scripture and you will find story after story of those who did not heed the advice given by prophets in the Old Testament. And the New Testament offers a wealth of admonitions and exhortations for those who would follow it. The parables of Jesus and his Sermon on the Mount offer the best advice.

In Mark 4:9, Jesus said, *"Whoever has ears to hear, let them hear."*

Much of the time we brush off well-meant advice because, as an old saying goes, "Advice would always be more acceptable if it didn't conflict with our plans."

Proverbs 19:21 reads, *"Many are the plans in a man's heart, but it is the Lord's purpose that prevails."*

Two centenarians, both female, were recently interviewed for a newspaper article. The two women were receiving a free hair-and-makeup session at a local upscale salon. At the end of the interview, the reporter asked one of the women if she had any advice to offer for living to 100. She replied, "Just leave it to God. He paves the way."

I think she has it right. Don't you?

Follow Through

Communicate: As mothers, we want the best for our children — no matter their age. We often feel like failures when they don't heed our advice. I have to remind myself sometimes that learning from their mistakes is the best teacher. Have you given your children any advice lately? Did they take it? How did they react to your advice? Were you disappointed in the results if they didn't take your advice? Why or why not? Journal your thoughts and emotions about the incident and let it go.

Cherish: Can you recall advice given to you by your mother or a trusted friend? What was it? If you listened to their advice, what was the outcome? Are you glad you chose to follow their advice? Why or why not? Again, write about the incident in your journal and cherish the memory.

Celebrate: Did you know resisting advice is natural? According to psychologist Thomas J. Mowbray, "Taking advice is not natural. It just seems obvious that any mature adult knows how to take advice. But in practice, people seldom do because is it not natural. Normally, everyone thinks that they know what they are doing and they can handle situations with the force of their own will. In a sense, people mistakenly assume they can control the world, even when they are in a brand-new situation where they don't have a clue "how things happen.""

Reread Mowbray's statement focusing on the last sentence.

Before I let Jesus have control of my life, I believed I could control the world or at least the outcome of things in my world. I tell others I was the poster child for control freaks. Now, I celebrate because He has set me free. What about you? Do you resist taking advice? Examine your answer in your journal.

WEEK 20

IS NORMAL JUST A SETTING
ON YOUR CLOTHES DRYER?

"Behold, children are a heritage from the Lord, the fruit of the womb a reward" — Psalm 127:3 (ESV).

"Normal is just a setting on your clothes dryer." I love this quote by author and speaker Patsy Clairmont. I've heard her speak several times at Women of Faith conferences and love her sense of humor.

As mothers, we must embrace a sense of humor if we want to survive the ups and downs of that most sacred role. We strive to be perfect mothers, i.e. normal, but we're all different. As women, we struggle, fail, start over and celebrate the small and large victories as we watch our children grow from a tiny bald-headed creature we fell in love with before he/she ever emerged from the womb to adulthood.

Motherhood, while celebrated, is not easy. I can attest to that. So can millions of other mothers. It's a role bringing joy, heartache and satisfaction to the one called "Mother."

A Jewish proverb says, "God could not be everywhere, so He created mothers." Can you relate?

One of the most often quoted scriptures on love is 1 Corinthians 13:4-7. *"Love is patient; love is kind. Love is not jealous; is not proud; is not conceited; does not act foolishly; is not selfish; is not easily provoked to anger; keeps no record of wrongs; takes no pleasure in unrighteousness, but rejoices in the truth; love bears all things, believes all things, hopes all things, and endures all things."*

As mothers we can love unlike any other person. Since my two sons have become men with children of their own, I've come to understand how God feels about us, His children.

Once our grown children leave home, they make choices we don't always agree with, but that doesn't stop us from loving them. We may be disappointed about some of their decisions, but we don't stop loving or praying for them.

Each morning, after my Bible study, I pray for all my loved ones, including my sons. Sometimes, it's difficult to know how to pray for others, especially for our adult children. We aren't always aware of what is happening in their lives, unless they choose to reveal it to us.

About five years ago, when both of my sons were going through some trials, I discovered a book called, *The Power of Praying for Your Adult Children*, a book of prayers by Stormie Omartian.

In the introduction to the book, the author says, "As long as we live, we parents will always have our children on our minds and hearts. Even after they become adults, we will forever be concerned for their safety, well-being, relationship with God, and success in all they do — from their work to their health, to their friends, to their marriage relationship, to the raising of their children."

Lamentations 2:19 tells us, *"Lift up your hands to Him for the lives of your children."*

While we celebrate mothers once a year on Mother's Day, most mothers celebrate their children every day. For me, that's normal.

Follow Through

Communicate: Growing up, I could not recall my mother ever saying, "I love you." But I never doubted her love because she demonstrated love in so many ways. She was a stay-at-home mom who sewed, making most of the clothing my sister and I wore. She cooked tasty, nutritious homemade meals. She sponsored our Blue Bird and Camp Fire Girl groups. She taught my sister and me the things we needed to know to be independent when we grew up and left home. However, I was in my late 40s before she said the words I longed to hear — "I love you."

Can you recall the first time your mother told you she loved you? If you never heard her say those words, did you ever doubt her love? Journal your thoughts and emotions about your mother and the relationship you have/had with her — whether she is still with you or not.

Cherish: I was 51 and had just become a grandmother several months before my mother passed away in 2004. When I was growing up, I can't recall her sharing many of her own childhood memories with us. However, when she was in her late 70s, she began to open up and share some of the things she recalled from her childhood growing up in northeastern Oklahoma. I treasure those stories.

Can you recall your mother sharing her childhood memories? If so, write them down to pass on to your children. If not and she's still alive, interview her about her life. You might want to record the stories. If you've never shared your childhood memories with your children, begin today. Write them down or record them.

Celebrate: Reflect on Charles Stanley's quote below about motherhood:

> "Motherhood is a great honor and privilege, yet it is also synonymous with servanthood. Every day women are called upon to selflessly meet the needs of their families. Whether they are awake at night nursing a baby, spending their time and money on less-than-grateful teenagers, or preparing meals, moms continuously put others before themselves."

What does motherhood mean to you? If you're not a mother, think about the sacrifices your mother made for you? Celebrate motherhood.

WEEK 21

THE POWER OF A PRAYING MOTHER

"For this child I prayed; and the Lord has granted me the petition that I made to him"— 1 Samuel 1:27(NRSV).

When a child is born, a mother anxiously checks for 10 fingers and 10 toes. She waits to hear the verdict from the medical staff that her child is healthy and whole. It's a time of wonder when that tiny being is first placed in your arms and a time of uncertainty when you're released to return home with the responsibilities of caring for a new life.

As each year passes, we watch our children grow, revealing their distinct personalities. While one child may be more fearful, another may test a mother's patience with attempts to defy gravity or some other activity leading to cuts, bruises and broken limbs.

As the mother of two sons, now in their late 30s, I am aware of the limitations of my influence at this stage of their lives. With the lessons they learned as children embedded in their memories, I can only pray daily for their safety, well-being, their relationship with God and success in all they do. I pray for their work situations, their health, their relationships and how they raise their children.

When a child is young, a mother knows how to fix things. We can kiss a scraped elbow, place a warm, damp wash rag on their heads to bring comfort when ill, listen to their fears and promise them there are no monsters under the bed.

A mother's heart is torn when a child becomes an adult and she realizes how her role has changed. Letting go is difficult.

In last week's devotional, I mentioned a small book of prayers by Stormie Omartian. My copy is now well-worn because I use it each morning during my quiet time with the Lord. I also write the date I prayed that prayer for each one of my sons.

In the introduction, the author writes, "I believe these prayers will help any parent to have a positive impact on the lives of their adult children. I pray that each prayer will help you to find greater freedom from worry and concern because you are tapping into the power of God, which is greater than anything you or they may be facing. When we take our concerns to the Lord—trusting that God hears our prayers and answers them on behalf of our adult children—our prayers will have the power to effect change in their lives."

The first prayer in the book is titled "What Every Parent of an Adult Child Needs to Know," reminding us that the Lord is the only perfect parent. Many of us blame ourselves for the mistakes we made when parenting our young children. This prayer reminded me I needed to confess my mistakes and ask God to redeem and release me from all my guilt.

Trusting God to work His will in my sons' lives has made this mother's heart peaceful.

Follow Through

Communicate: Do you have adult children? If so, do you pray for them? Have you seen your prayers answered? Don't become discouraged if you don't see answers right away. Do you find yourself anxious, even after you have prayed? Are you turning your adult children over to God? If not, now is the time to do so. Write out your concerns for your adult children and/or praise the Lord for answering your prayers concerning them.

Cherish: We can cherish the memories of when our children were young and we could "fix" their problems. Once they become adults, it's often difficult to let go. I know it was for me. It has been a growing process for me to trust God with the lives of my sons.

Since I began using Stormie's book of prayers, my load has grown lighter. Stormie says, "I pray that each prayer will help you to find greater freedom from worry and concern because you are tapping into the power of God, which is greater than anything you or they may be facing."

Take your concerns about your adult children to the Lord in prayer. Be sure to document in your journal when you see changes in their lives. Be sure and date your prayers and the answers.

Celebrate: Look up and write down *1 John 5:14-15* on an index card and keep it with your journal to remind you God is faithful to answer our prayers according to His will.

June

Discover, Delight, Devote

"Delight yourself in the LORD, and he will give you the desires of your heart"—Psalm 37:4 (ESV).

What are the desires of your heart? What does it mean to delight yourself in the Lord? Does it mean we will receive everything our heart wants?

Recently, I came across an article by Jen Pollock Michel in *Relevant* magazine. Titled "What We Get Wrong About the 'Desires of Our Heart,'" the article was an eye-opener for me.

Michel's article began with a question posed by a visiting pastor in the pulpit one day. He asked, "How many of you have prayed, 'God, help me to love you more?'"

Michel confessed silently that she has prayed the prayer ritually for 20 years. She says, "Those words were my desperate, white-knuckled grip on grace—because, like the Prodigal Son, I knew about loving something and someone other than God."

However, Michel says she was surprised when the pastor added, "If you've prayed, 'God, help me to love you more,' you're praying the wrong thing. You should be praying, 'God, help me to know you more.'"

Michel, however, disagreed with this young pastor. "It's not that I don't love theology. I do. I believe in the great good that good doctrine can do as it teaches us about God, about the world, about ourselves. Every day, in fact, I read the Bible to know more of God."

She continued:

"But for all of this accumulated knowing about God, never do I entrust myself to the foolhardy certainty that 'knowing things' is a talisman, warding off temptation and threat. My spiritual problems, in fact, seem less related to what I don't know and more related to what I don't love. Among Christians, we often hear that God will give us 'the desires of our hearts.' And it's true that God cares about our innermost desires, but often, we need His intervention to shape those most important desires, including our desire for Him.

"Every one of us needs to be praying, 'God, help me to love you more.' "

In June, we'll discover more about ourselves and our relationship with our Heavenly Father, learning to delight in Him and devote ourselves to loving Him even more.

WEEK 22

HE CHOSE YOU FIRST

Jesus said, "You didn't choose me, but I chose you"—John 15:16 (CEB).

I recall a conversation between two of my grandchildren while we were eating supper. It brought back childhood memories of my own.

My youngest grandson, Cash, was starting school that year. He missed the cut-off date by two days the previous year, so he was probably one of the older ones in his pre-kindergarten class. I'm guessing he'd also be one of the tallest as he's always been big for his age.

As we ate our supper, we began discussing the upcoming school year. Brennan, my oldest grandson who was nine at the time, began to give advice to his younger cousin. The talk turned to bullying when Brennan said, "Cash, if you're the smallest in your class, people will pick on you."

My heart went out to him because I knew Brennan spoke from experience. He's one of the smallest in his class. However, as Brennan began to explain to his cousin how he dealt with bullies, I had to smile. I knew God was working in my grandson's life because I was seeing evidence of my answered prayers as Brennan spoke. I listened, and then said, "Do you know why bullies pick on others, especially smaller people?"

I had their attention as I continued. "They do so to make themselves feel better. They're usually not happy with their own lives and sometimes it's not their fault. They could come from a home where they're not loved. Picking on someone smaller than they are makes them feel they're in control."

I, too, was picked on when I was in elementary school. Not only was I small for my age, but I wasn't athletic, which meant I was one of the last ones chosen for playground games, like Kick Ball and Red Rover.

Because of my own childhood experiences, I could empathize with Brennan, who's now finding his niche on the basketball court as a guard. He's small but aggressive on the court.

The following morning, as my grandchildren were playing, I was spending time with the Lord in my sunroom. I was reading a daily devotional in *The Upper Room* when I realized the message fit the previous evening's conversation.

In the devotional, written by a man in Pennsylvania, he shared his own experiences with being chosen last. Because he was the new kid in town and the smallest in his neighborhood, he was the last one chosen when teams were formed to play baseball. As I finished reading the author's story, I knew I needed to share it with my grandsons.

Calling them into the sunroom, I shared that day's scripture, John 15:16, and the devotional that followed. My grandsons both listened intently as I read the devotional aloud and then said, "Do you know what that means?"

I reread the scripture: "Jesus said, *'You didn't choose me, but I chose you.'*"

Brennan said, "It means Jesus loves us."

Cash chimed in. "Yes, Jesus loves us."

Yes, Jesus loves us. Regardless of our size or abilities, He'll always choose us.

Follow Through

Discover: How does it feel knowing that Jesus chose you first? If you were not chosen first for teams (or if you were chosen last) during your school years, does this scripture bring you a sense of belonging and peace? What would you tell your younger self now about being last?

Delight: Meditate on the word "delight." Journal your ideas and then look up the word in a dictionary. Does your definition reflect the meaning as found in the dictionary?

Devote: Devote yourself this week to loving God more by sharing His Love with the unlovable in your life—whether it is a family member, neighbor, co-worker or acquaintance.

WEEK 23

WHAT'S SO AMAZING ABOUT GRACE?

"For it is by grace you have been saved, through faith—and this is not from yourselves, it is the gift of God— not by works, so that no one can boast"—Ephesians 2:8-9 (NIV).

It seems a cowboy from Colorado skipped church one Sunday to go bear hunting in the mountains. As he turned the corner along the path, he and a bear collided. The cowboy stumbled backwards, slipped off the trail and began tumbling down the mountain with the bear in hot pursuit. Finally, the cowboy crashed into a boulder, sending his rifle in one direction and breaking both legs.

As the bear closed in, the cowboy cried out in desperation, "Lord, I'm sorry for what I have done. Please forgive me and save me! Lord, please make that bear a Christian."

Suddenly, the clouds parted and a beam of light shone down on the bear. The bear skidded to a halt at the cowboy's feet, fell to its knees, clasped its paws together and said, "God, bless this food which I am about to receive."

While we can laugh at this joke, how many of us fail to grasp the breadth of God's amazing grace? One scripture holds the answer. John 3:16 says, *"For God so loved the world, that He gave His only begotten Son, that whoever believes in Him shall not perish, but have eternal life."*

One of my favorite hymns is "Amazing Grace." Slave trader John Newton, a man deeply entrenched in sin, penned the song in 1773 after he experienced the transforming power of God's grace during a violent storm at sea.

During the Civil War, both sides sang the song and on the Trail of Tears, the Cherokee Indians used it as a requiem for their dead. Civil Rights protestors defiantly sang it during Freedom Marches.

When Nelson Mandela was freed from prison and when the Berlin Wall came tumbling down, "Amazing Grace" rang out. A mourning world sang the lyrics on September 11, 2001 and when the New Orleans Saints marched back into the Superdome after Hurricane Katrina, reviving the spirit of a fallen city.

In 1 Timothy 1:15, Paul wrote: *"It is a trustworthy statement, deserving full acceptance, that Christ Jesus came into the world to save sinners, among whom I am foremost of all."*

What's so amazing about His grace? Christian author Regina Franklin has this to say about grace. "His grace should cause us to be speechless before Him. The temptation comes, however, either to make God no more significant than the latest thrill or to view Him as noticeably distant and cruelly authoritative.

"A consuming fire" (Hebrews 12:29), He does not desire our destruction but burns away anything that would destroy us. His work in our lives reminds us that we are not God. Rather than quaking in fear, however, we bow with steady knees and reach with confident arms. May we live with a palpable sense of His incredible power, brilliant holiness, and genuine goodness."

Grace—we don't deserve it. We can't earn it. It's a gift. Isn't that amazing?

Follow Through

Discover: Have you discovered God's amazing grace? In your journal, write down John 3:16. Meditate on the scripture, picturing Jesus hanging on the cross.

Delight: My favorite definition for God's grace is "God giving us what we don't deserve." While we deserved the punishment of Hell, God graciously bestowed on us the gift of His Son. Grace. What does it mean to you? How have you seen God's grace exhibited in your daily life? Where? How?

Devote: How can you become more devoted to showing God's grace to others? Make a list of people that come to mind. What can you do for others to exhibit God's grace? Here are some suggestions from author

David Peach at https://www.whatchristianswanttoknow.com:

1. *Show grace when you speak by using words that are kind.* Even when we need to correct others, we can find a way to say it in gentle way.
2. *Look for the needs of others.* If we seek opportunities, like holding a door open for someone, we become a grace-giver.
3. *Respond with grace when you are criticized, even unjustly.* Accept what the other person has to say and thank them for their input. Responding in anger doesn't diffuse the situation.
4. *Offer your graceful presence.* Take opportunities to be with someone who is grieving the loss of a loved one. Even if you only have 10 minutes to spare, stopping by to say hello can mean the world to those who are experiencing a death in the family.
5. *Forgive with grace.* When someone asks for forgiveness, how do you react? Do you accept their apology graciously or do you try to correct them, reminding them how wrong they were?
6. *Learn to say, "I'm sorry."* On the other hand, when you make a mistake, swallow your pride and ask for forgiveness. Maybe the other person was wrong, but you responded in an inappropriate manner. (I've been there and done that.) But, after thinking about it, I've apologized for my response, even if the other person didn't deserve it. You're asking for forgiveness for your response.
7. *Keep short accounts.* When you apologize, do it quickly. Don't keep a tally of how many times the other person has wronged you. Forgive, even if they don't ask for it. Grace goes a long way toward repairing a relationship.
8. *Say "thank you" to show grace to others.* When we express our gratitude to others, whether it's thanking a waiter or your best friend, others want to know they are appreciated. I love writing thank you notes to friends and family members to show my appreciation for a kind act on my behalf.
9. *Take an interest in others.* When you're introduced to a new person, ask questions. Show an interest in others, not by being nosy, but by showing a genuine respect for the other person, even if you don't think you'll ever meet him or her again. But, if you do, I can guarantee they will remember you as a person who showed them grace.
10. *What else can you do to show grace to others?* Make a list in your journal.

WEEK 24

YOU'VE GOT 86,400 SECONDS

"But your hearts must be fully committed to the Lord our God, to live by his decrees and obey his commands, as at this time"—1 Kings 8:61 (NIV).

I'm in my sixth decade of living. Recently, I told a friend that even if I had several hundred years to live, I would never be able to reach all of the goals I have set for myself. I realize, however, that my goals may not be the same as God's plans for my life, and I'm okay with that.

The following poem, often recited by Dr. Benjamin Elijah Mays, is about squeezing value out of the time God has given each of us. We often forget, however, that our time on earth is a gift from our Heavenly Father. It is for our use, but it is limited to the number of days we live.

> I've only just a minute,
> Only sixty seconds in it.
> Forced upon me, can't refuse it,
> Didn't seek it, didn't choose it,
> But it's up to me to use it.
> I must suffer if I lose it.
> Give an account if I abuse it,
> Just a tiny little minute,
> But eternity is in it.

Born in 1894 to former slaves, Mays was inspired by Frederick Douglas, Paul Laurence Dunbar and Booker T. Washington. He became a Baptist minister, earned a Ph.D. from the University of Chicago, served as Dean of the Howard University School of Religion, was an advisor to several United States presidents, served as a member and as President of the Atlanta Board of Education, and was President of Morehouse College for 27 years. In addition to his own vast accomplishments, Mays was an inspiration and advisor to his students, including Dr. Martin Luther King, Jr., who referred to Dr. Mays as his "spiritual mentor."

Dr. Mays, commenting on our mission, said, "All around you in this broken world, people are suffering. So many unmet needs exist that it can all seem overwhelming. But it's not naïve to think that you can make a significant and lasting difference for the better. As a Christian, God calls you to do so, by representing Jesus in the world. God doesn't intend for you to shrink back from the needs around you; He wants to use your life to help others. In fact, God has uniquely created you to meet certain needs and is hoping you'll accept your mission."

To accomplish our mission, we must imagine our day as a bank account. If we are credited each morning with $86,400, but it carries over no balance from day to day, and every evening cancels whatever amount we have failed to use during the day, we'd draw out every cent. Everyone has such a bank account but it is credited with time, 86,400 seconds every morning. Every night it writes off, as lost, whatever of this time you have failed to invest to good purpose.

As each year passes, I feel the urgent need to invest my time wisely. How are you spending your 86,400 seconds?

Follow Through

Discover: As we celebrate each birthday, we are one day closer to the end of our life. That thought should make us appreciate each minute, hour, day and year we are on this earth. Does that thought create a sense of urgency in you? Why or why not?

Delight: German Lutheran pastor and theologian, Dietrich Bonhoeffer once said, "Time is lost when we have not lived a full human life, time unenriched by experience, creative endeavor, enjoyment, and suffering." Have you been living a full human life? How has your life been enriched by experiences? Creative endeavors? Enjoyment? What do you think Bonhoeffer meant about suffering as part of living a full human life?

Devote: Reread Dr. Mays' quote above about our mission in the world. What can you do to help eliminate the suffering in the world? Have you already found a mission field? How are you serving? What do you think God has uniquely created you to do in this world? Are you doing it? Devote your time to figuring it out and then follow through.

WEEK 25

HELP ME LORD, I NEED SOME DIRECTION

"But the plans of the Lord stand firm forever, the purposes of his heart through all generations"—Psalm 33:11 (NIV).

Have you ever been lost? I have. I'm not only directionally challenged but I can get lost with a GPS, especially if I ignore the "voice" giving me orders to go right or turn left.

Our relationship with God can be just like that. We can get lost in the cacophony of a noisy world shouting, "Follow me. I've got all the answers," or "If you buy this gadget/book/pill, your life will be transformed in three easy steps."

While following God is not always easy, His path is clear. Psalm 16:11 says, *"You make known to me the path of life; you will fill me with joy in your presence, with eternal pleasures at your right hand."*

Determining God's path for my life came only after I surrendered my will to His. I did not invite Him to be the Lord of every breath I take until I was in my late 40s. I can still recall that peaceful fall afternoon in 2001 when I prayed aloud for the first time.

My prayer that day was heartfelt and born out of desperation. "God, please help me. I need some direction in my life."

Since that day, almost 16 years ago, I have been seeking His guidance, His plans and His goals for my life. Have I gotten it right every time? No. However, my prayer journal entries reveal a woman who has grown closer to Him, a woman who has learned to trust that "still, small voice," often drowned by the outside world. Keeping a prayer journal has helped me to distinguish between the world's shouts and His quiet whisper, telling me to go this way or that.

I recall a journal entry in July 2003 when I was considering a job change. Although I had been encouraged by friends to apply for the position, I was uncertain. I was only two years from retirement.

However, the new job, if I was hired, would mean substantially more money and a heftier retirement check. I was not afraid of change, but I had been a part of the faculty for 28 years in the same school system. I didn't have peace about the change, even if others were encouraging me to apply. I did apply, trusting that God was in charge and not me.

On the morning of my scheduled interview, I read Proverbs 3:5-6 before journaling my prayer to God.

> *"Trust in the Lord with all your heart*
> *And lean not on your own understanding;*
> *in all your ways acknowledge Him,*
> *and He will make your paths straight."*

Immediately, I felt a peace settle around my soul. Whatever the outcome of my interview, I knew God was in control. I praised God in my journal for making His presence known to me that morning.

The interview went well. In fact, it was probably the best I'd ever experienced. Maybe that's because I was trusting God for the outcome. While I didn't get the job, I knew God's plans for me were much better than I could ever imagine.

If you're struggling with identifying His plans for your life, try writing a letter to Him in your journal. Ask Him to show you the way. He will. You just have to trust that still, small voice. He won't lead you astray.

Follow Through

Discover: Have you ever been lost? Are you directionally challenged? Recall a time when you were lost. How did you find your way? What about in your spiritual life? Did God help you find your way? How?

Delight: Delight yourself in the scriptures that bring peace to a weary soul. Commit to memorizing those that speak to your heart. Proverbs 3:5-6 has become a soul-satisfying one for me when I need direction and guidance.

Devote: If you don't already set aside morning time with the Lord, make a commitment to do so. Even if your time frame is only 10 minutes, it's a beginning. Seek Him in reading a scripture each day. A good place to start is with the Psalms. Highlight those that speak to your heart. Read the highlighted scriptures aloud and feel the words seep into the very inner part of your being.

Copy onto index cards those scriptures you want to memorize. Carry them in your purse or post them around your house as a reminder to seek Him always.

WEEK 26

GUESS HOW MUCH HE LOVES YOU

"I pray that out of his glorious riches, he may strengthen you with power through his Spirit in your inner being, so that Christ may dwell in your hearts through faith. And I pray that you, being rooted and established in love may have power together with all the Lord's holy people, to grasp how wide and long and high and deep is the love of Christ"— Ephesians 3:16-18(NIV).

Do you remember your first love? Maybe you were in grade school. Maybe it was junior high. Even if you can't remember your age, you probably remember the feeling.

You wanted him or her to notice you. Maybe you picked a flower and pulled the petals off one-by-one and chanted, "He loves me. He loves me not. He loves me. He loves me not. He loves me. He loves me not . . ."—oh, just one more petal please. Disappointed, you threw the treacherous stem to the ground.

But then you grew up—hopefully—to realize love can't be measured by the number of petals on a flower.

I can remember when my sons were young. We would play a game. They would ask me, "Mama, how much do you love us?"

I would hold my hands about two feet apart and say, "This is how much I love you."

"Is that all?"

I'd laugh and move my hands farther apart. Again, they would ask, "Is that all, Mama?"

This game would continue until my arms would stretch as far as they could. Then, I would reply. "My love for you can't be measured."

I now have six grandchildren. I think the sweetest words I have ever heard are, "I love you Nana."

I love buying books for my grandchildren. One of my favorites to read when they were younger is the classic, *Guess How Much I Love You?*

The story's plot revolves around Little Nutbrown Hare asking Big Nutbrown Hare, "Guess how much I love you?" to which he replies, "Oh, I don't think I could guess that."

As the little hare uses different ways to show how much he loves Big Nutbrown Hare, the older rabbit always replies with a demonstration of his own love. By the last page, we find out that the little hare's love for the bigger hare is very hard to measure.

At the end of the story, the little hare looks out into the dark night and says, "I love you right up to the moon," to which the big hare replies, "That is very, very far."

As the little rabbit drifts off to sleep, Big Nutbrown Hare leans over and kisses him good night. His final words are, "I love you right up to the moon—and back."

How much can you love someone? We don't have to guess how much we are loved by God. We can fall asleep at night secure that His love for us is beyond measure.

Can you grasp how wide and long and high and deep is the love of Christ? Look at the cross. See his outstretched arms. Guess how much He loves you.

Follow Through

Discover: Have you ever felt the love of God enfolding you in His arms? I have. To me, it feels like a warm blanket covering me in peace. What did it feel like to you?

Delight: Use a concordance to look up and copy into your journal the scriptures that express God's love for His people. Did you know those scriptures apply to you too? Which one speaks to you the most? Why?

Devote: For those you know who've never experienced the unconditional love of our Heavenly Father, how would you explain it to them? Find someone this week that needs to feel His love and share it with them. Then, journal the experience.

July

Feed, Focus, Flourish

"So let's keep focused on that goal, those of us who want everything God has for us. If any of you have something else in mind, something less than total commitment, God will clear your blurred vision - you'll see it yet!" — Philippians 3:15 (MSG).

W hat does it mean to grow in grace? In 2 Peter 3:18, Christians are told to *"grow in the grace and knowledge of the Lord Jesus Christ."* To grow in grace is to mature as a Christian.

We are saved by grace through faith and we mature and are sanctified by grace alone. It's a blessing we don't deserve. God's grace justifies us, sanctifies us, and eventually glorifies us in heaven. Becoming more like Christ is synonymous with growing in grace.

How do we grow in grace? First, we need to feed on God's Holy Word, letting it "dwell in us richly" (Colossians 3:16). Second, we must spend time in prayer.

 While these actions alone don't bring maturity, God uses these spiritual disciplines to help us grow. Therefore, maturing in our Christian life is not about what we do, but about what God does in us, by His grace.

When we begin to understand and apply God's grace in our lives, we are strengthened to break free of our sinful nature and follow Him. His grace protects us. Without the amazing grace of our Heavenly Father, we would be hopelessly lost.

To grow in grace does not mean we gain more grace from God. He gave His only Son so that whoever believes in Him should be saved

(John 3:16). How much more grace could there possibly be than the sacrifice of His only Son on the cross?

To become more grace-filled is to grow in our understanding of what Jesus did for each of us. The more we learn about Jesus, the more we begin to appreciate all He has done. The more we appreciate His love and sacrifice for us, the more we will understand the never-ending grace of God.

If we want to have a more intimate relationship with our Savior and experience all God's grace has to offer, we need to focus on increasing our knowledge of Jesus. By growing in God's grace, we will flourish, thrive and be transformed into the image of His Son.

In July, we'll discover the freedom of becoming the person God created us to be by focusing on growing in grace.

WEEK 27

YOU HAVE THE FREEDOM TO CHOOSE

"It is for freedom that Christ has set us free. Stand firm, then, and do not let yourselves be burdened again by a yoke of slavery"—Galatians 5:1 (NIV).

For more years than I care to count, I was a slave. No one held me captive behind bars. Loss of freedom was my own choice.

However, I was in my late 40s before I realized I could choose freedom. I had allowed the opinions of others, and my own desire to please others, to hold me hostage. When I disappointed others, I felt guilty and inadequate.

Most people were unaware of my insecurities. People who didn't know me very well thought I had my life together. I did on the outside. I worked hard at putting on a mask of perfection.

I became an overachiever, seeking accomplishments and accolades to bolster my self-esteem. After reaching the top of the ladder in my profession, I felt nothing, except a gnawing emptiness.

Despite my achievements, I felt incomplete and often wished I were someone else. I thought if I performed well or appeared attractive on the outside, it would carry over into my internal life. I didn't know I could only find an inner peace that comes from knowing who you really are in Christ.

After my Savior set me free, I came to realize the real meaning in life is not the product of what you have or don't have, or what you've done or haven't done. Because I am a child of God, I am already a whole person with a life of meaning and purpose.

As my relationship with Him has grown, so has my freedom to make choices. In the past, when I was asked to take on a task, I would not only tackle the job, but also excel at it. Often, my decision to accept the offer was based on flattery that I had been chosen to do the job. I thought I had to continue to prove myself.

God loves us so much that He gave us the freedom to make choices. Although some are of little consequence, others are life-changing. We have all made poor choices. However, there is good news because no matter our past, there is always hope for a better future.

Recently, I overheard a conversation at a local store. An elderly woman was in a handicapped cart, while a younger woman, whom I presumed to be her daughter, was juggling children, an overflowing grocery cart and a calculator.

As one of the children begged his mother for a toy, she was going through the cart taking an inventory of its contents. When the child continued to plead, she snapped at him. The older woman reproached her and the mother replied, "I have no choice. I've never had a choice."

I didn't know her history but my heart went out to her because we do have choices and the most important choice we can ever make is to choose freedom through a relationship with the Lord.

Have you made that choice?

Follow Through

Feed: What feeds your spirit? Is it the opinions of others? Is it your accomplishments? Honestly examine your thoughts in your journal.

Focus: Where do you focus your thoughts each day? Is your focus on making a good impression or is it on helping others? If your insecurities are keeping you locked in a prison, what can you do to break free? Make a list of activities that will challenge you to get outside your comfort zone and reach out to others. Ask the Holy Spirit to help you break free from whatever is holding you captive.

Flourish: Reread Galatians 5:1 and remind yourself what Christ did on the cross to set you free. He came to give His followers an abundant life, filled with His amazing grace. Have you accepted His gift? What does that mean to you?

WEEK 28

CHANGE REQUIRES EFFORT
AND A WHOLE LOT OF JESUS

"Jesus Christ is the same yesterday and today and forever"—Hebrews 13:8(NIV).

"The only one who likes change is a wet baby." I chuckled when I read this quote. I don't know who said it but it's the truth. Change is never easy because it requires us to leave our comfort zone, that place where we feel we are in control.

Giving up control is not painless. This does not mean we give up responsibility for our words and actions; it means giving up control of those things over which we really have no control.

I used to be the poster child for control freaks. Then, things began to happen in my life—events I could not control, things I could not fix, people I could not change.

But Jesus got ahold of me and I began to change. Change requires effort. Some of us are dragged, kicking and screaming through the forces of change. Others are led gently by the hand, if we surrender.

When those we think we know and can trust disappoint us, we must change our attitude or risk a life of constant frustration because we can change no one but ourselves. Once we accept this fact of life, life becomes less complicated. Living a less complicated life is easier—once you get the hang of it.

It can take a lifetime to get the hang of it though. We think we have conquered that nasty little beast called "being in control" and then, lo and behold, it rears its ugly head in the form of fear and nips us in the bottom while we aren't looking. Ouch, that hurts!

Being a control freak causes pain, not only for us but for others as well.

We have to accept and celebrate the fact that we are all different. Kobi Yamada, President/CEO of Compendium Incorporated, a publishing and strategic communications company, once said, "Embrace your uniqueness. Time is much too short to be living someone else's life."

He's right. Instead of wasting time trying to change those people/things over which we have no control, we should be focusing on our purpose while we are here on earth. I like Yamada's personal mission statement: "One by one, we can be the better world we wish for."

His statement is simple but so profound. When we focus on our talents and gifts and what we have to offer the world, we let go of the need to change others to fit our mold. The only one who can change us is us—with the help of a whole lot of Jesus.

Through a relationship with the Lord, we can allow Him to change us—our bad habits and our bad attitudes. Releasing the desire to be in control to the One who is in control is not easy. When we turn to Him, the one who is the same—yesterday, today and forever—then we have taken the first step toward living a life that really matters.

Can you release your need to be in control? Let the One who is really in control show you how.

Follow Through

Feed: How would you define a control freak? Would you say you are one? Why or why not? If you're not sure, ask a trusted friend. Some-times we don't recognize the need to be in control. I didn't until my world spiraled out of control.

Focus: If you're like me—or how I used to be—you crave control. What's the cure for being a control freak? Can you change without the help of the Holy Spirit? Why or why not? Spend time with God, be honest and tell Him how you feel.

In an article by Lauren Gaskill at ibelieve.com, she offers the following prayer to help you begin to let go and let God:

"God I confess I like being in control. It makes me feel safe and secure. It makes me feel like I have a purpose. But I know that being a control freak isn't going to get me anywhere. Help me surrender control to you each and every day. Help me trust in you deeply, so that I will not fear surrendering that control. Help me remember that you hold it all."

Gaskill adds, "If you're having trouble surrendering through prayer alone, try taking out a piece of paper and writing down the things you are holding so tightly to. One by one, lay the pieces of paper on the floor and as you're doing so, imagine yourself literally laying them down at the feet of the Father."

Flourish: Until we surrender our need to be in charge of the universe—or at least our part of the world—we'll never become the woman He has created us to be. Surrendering to God's sovereignty is a lifelong journey. It's not a "stick-it-in-the-microwave and zap it" process. It requires us to be intentional. It's a choice we make each day. When we learn to let go of trying to figure out the "whys" of life, we begin to trust our Heavenly Father who understands more than we ever can.

Surrender control. Wait. Trust in God's plan. Jeremiah 29:13 says *"You will find Me when you search for Me with all your heart"* (NASB).

Make a list in your journal of the times God has carried you through the tough times. Know He will continue to be faithful to lead you where He wants you to go.

WEEK 29

ARE YOU JUST 'DOING' THE BIBLE?

"I came so they can have real and eternal life, more and better life than they ever dreamed of"—John 10:10 (MSG).

Have you ever asked yourself, "How did I get here?"

When you're lost, whether it's physically, emotionally or spiritually, maybe it's time to stop and reassess where you are. While reading a recent Q & A interview with author Bob Goff, I was intrigued with his response to the following question: "Why did you trade in 'Bible study' for 'Bible doing' and what's the difference?"

Goff said, "I love reading scripture and find tremendous comfort and perspective in exploring God's Word. However, I stopped going to Bible studies a while ago. Instead, I go to a 'Bible doing.'"

Since I had never encountered the term, "Bible doing," I wanted to know more. Goff explains the concept by saying he spent the first couple of decades of his faith in Bible studies, getting together with others, reading the Bible and talking about what words meant in Greek and Latin.

In addition, the group would discuss the customs, culture and surroundings at the time as well as the origins of certain words. As a trial lawyer by training, Goff was a man who memorized facts well.

"So when I went to Bible studies," he says, "I'd just memorize more and more facts about Jesus."

Goff could tell you all about Jesus' mom, where He grew up, what He had for dinner, every wedding or event He showed up at and how many boats were on the Sea of Galilee. However, he says, "Honestly, I didn't know Him."

Goff adds, "I think it was because we never actually did anything together. I was just too busy memorizing Him. What I realized is that I had become a lot like a stalker—someone who just collects facts and information about people they're too scared to meet."

What Goff soon realized is that "by just memorizing Jesus, I had actually turned into kind of a stalker. What I concluded is that Jesus doesn't want us to just memorize Him. He wants us to experience life with and through Him."

Since that day, Goff doesn't do Bible studies. He still gets together with the same group but now they call it a "Bible doing."

He says, "The difference between the two is more than just a turn on a phrase. What we do now is read scripture and ask ourselves what we're actually going to do about it. Jesus never asked His disciples to agree with Him. Instead, He told them to take all of the faith they had, all of the scripture they knew and go do something about it. We want to do the same."

Although memorizing facts and scripture can be beneficial, if we don't do something with our faith, of what value is the first? In John 10:10, Jesus says, *"I came so they can have real and eternal life, more and better life than they ever dreamed of."*

Don't just read and study scripture. Begin "doing" the Bible.

Follow Through

Feed: Do you know Jesus or do you just know about Him? Have you, like Bob Goff, just memorized facts about Jesus? Reread today's devotional and ask yourself, "Am I just doing the Bible?"

Journal your thoughts and ask the Holy Spirit to help you to be honest with your reply about your relationship with your Savior.

Have you ever been lost? Not physically, but spiritually. How did you know you were lost? What precipitated the feeling of being lost?

Focus: Do you have a small study group? How long have you been a part of the group? Do you think it has helped you to draw closer to Jesus? Why or why not? How can you focus on growing closer to Jesus? In your journal, make a list of those things that would help you to draw closer to Him. Ask for Jesus' help in the process of discovery.

Flourish: Jesus told His disciples to take all of the faith they had, all of the scripture they knew and go do something about it. What can you do today, next week, or next month to begin "doing" the Bible?

In your journal, write down this prayer to Jesus:

Dear Jesus,

I don't want to just memorize scripture. I want to experience life with and through You. I need Your help Jesus to know you fully. I don't want to just do a Bible study. I want to read scripture and ask myself, "What am I going to do about it?"

Put your pen down, get quiet and tune into that still, small voice. Let Him lead you into "doing" the Bible.

WEEK 30

GOD DOES ALLOW U-TURNS

"Many are the plans in a person's heart, but it is the Lord's purpose that prevails"—Proverbs 19:21 (NIV).

A 2,000 mile journey to the east coast in 2012, taught me some valuable lessons. A friend and I, both of us directionally-challenged, left northeastern Oklahoma equipped with an atlas, MapQuest driving directions and my new GPS, which I dubbed "Shirley."

Don't ask me why I chose that name, it just popped in my head while we were on our road trip to Atlanta, Georgia. "Shirley" did not come with extensive written operating instructions. Although simpler is better in some cases, this woman, meaning me, is not tech-savvy.

I even went to the manufacturer's website before our June 15 departure to get detailed directions for "her" use. I also made three trips to the store where I had purchased the instrument prior to the departure date for assistance with "Shirley."

I know the clerks were probably laughing at a woman who prefers a Rand-McNally map in her hands to a female voice telling her to go right, go left or to make a U-turn when she doesn't listen.

I'm certain God is disappointed, and sometimes entertained, by our human tendency to ignore His voice. I can just hear Him saying, "Why don't you listen, my child? Things would be so much easier if you would just pay attention to my directions."

I'm also certain God allows U-turns when we get off the path He has planned for us. Even when we ignore that still, small voice telling us to go right and then turn left, He gently corrects us, leading us back on the right path if we are open. Did you know God speaks to you if you will only listen?

How do we listen? First, we must come to God and surrender our will. For me, a recovering control freak, the process is still sometimes a struggle. However, I have discovered that by taking it one day at a time, and sometimes one minute at a time, it's easier to lean on Him for direction.

I've also learned that surrendering control to Him frees me to become the woman He wants me to be. Surrender has a negative connotation in man's vocabulary. Not so in God's dictionary. God's definition equates surrender with freedom.

It takes courage to walk in freedom. One of the antonyms, or the opposite of the word freedom, is captivity. While we may not be locked behind bars, we can still be a prisoner of our own poor choices.

Musician David Stephens once said, "Freedom is the fragrance of grace."

God's grace frees us from the invisible chains holding us from His best. When we choose to follow His path, our lives are transformed into something better, even in the things we have imagined, expected, or hoped for.

Proverbs 3:5-6 says, *"Trust in the Lord with all your heart and lean not on your own understanding; in all your ways acknowledge Him, and He will make your paths straight."*

Following God's path for your life is rewarding. Do you know where you are going? He does allow U-turns.

Follow Through

Feed: Look up the definition of surrender in a dictionary or online? Does surrender have a negative connotation for you? Why or why not? What does it mean to surrender to God? Have you done that? What happened?

When I surrendered my plans, God led me on paths I had never dreamed of traveling. I've been on three mission trips, including two out of the country. I've also been to the Holy Land, where I walked in the footsteps of Jesus and traveled across the Sea of Galilee on a wooden boat.

What mission trips or adventures might you take if you fully surrendered to God? What has the Holy Spirit placed on your heart about serving Jesus? Do you need to surrender to Him to accomplish those things?

Focus: Have you experienced times when you know you've disappointed God? Why did you ignore that still, small voice? What happened?

As I've grown in my walk with Jesus, I've learned—the hard way—to pay attention to His voice and where it is leading me. Do I always get it right? No, but I am a work-in-progress. So are you. Don't beat yourself up when you make a wrong turn. Just turn to the One who loves you and seek His guidance. He allows U-turns.

Flourish: Think about the apostle Paul's U-turn in life as revealed in Acts 9. He thought he was headed in the right direction. He thought he was following God. But God intervened and turned his life around on the road to Damascus. It was there that he met Jesus and Paul's life was never the same.

Read Acts 9. Has God done anything dramatic in your life to get your attention and put you back on the right path—the path leading to everlasting life? If so, include the story in your journal and be ready to share with others about your U-turn when the opportunity arises.

August

Eliminate, Enlist, Enrich

"Two are better than one, because they have a good return for their labor: If either of them falls down, one can help the other up. But pity anyone who falls and has no one to help them up"— Ecclesiastes 4:9-10 (NIV).

What does friendship mean to you? According to *Webster's Dictionary*, a friend is "a person attached to another by feelings of affection or personal regard."

With the proliferation of social media, especially Facebook, we can have thousands of "friends." However, if we look at Webster's definition more closely, we might ask, "Are these real friendships?"

I'm blessed to have over 4,000 friends on Facebook. However, I could count on two hands the number whom I consider "true" friends. I must confess if someone who has "friended" me starts posting material I consider offensive or a waste of time, I select the "unfollow" button.

The same goes for "friends" who drag us down. What do I mean? Have you ever had someone you considered a friend who constantly complained, belittled others or gossiped about them? I have.

While I can pray for the individual, I don't want that person to drag me down with negativity. I was "that" person before Jesus got ahold of me and I have no desire to slip into old habits.

One of the first scriptures I memorized was Psalm 141:3. *"Set a guard over my mouth, Lord; keep watch over the door of my lips" (NIV).*

In 1 Corinthians 5:13 says, *"Do not be deceived: 'Bad company ruins good morals.'"*

~100~

Other scriptures warning us about the friends we choose include:

Proverbs 22:24-25 says, *"Do not make friends with a hot-tempered person, do not associate with one easily angered, or you may learn their ways and get yourself ensnared."*

Proverbs 12:26 reads, *"The righteous choose their friends carefully, but the way of the wicked leads them astray."*

We should seek friends who will help us to grow spiritually, who tell us the truth in love and who will be there when we need them. The reverse is also true. We should be a friend who possesses these qualities.

Proverbs 27:17 says, *"As iron sharpens iron, so one person sharpens another."*

So, how can we eliminate distractions from our lives and enlarge our circle of Godly friends who will enrich our lives as we enrich theirs? In August, we will examine our friendships with others and what it means to be a friend.

WEEK 31

WHAT DOES IT MEAN TO BE A FRIEND?

"A friend loves at all times, and a brother is there for times of trouble"—Proverbs17:17 (ISV).

What does it mean to be a friend? Recently, I heard a pastor describe it this way.

"A friend is a treasure who loves you as you are, sees not only who you are but who you can become, is there to catch you when you fall, shares your everyday experiences, accepts your worst but helps you become your best, understands your past, believes in your future, accepts you today just as you are, and comes in when the whole world has gone out."

Proverbs 17:17 puts it this way. *"A friend loves at all times, and a brother is there for times of trouble."* In this case, brother doesn't necessarily mean a blood relative. Instead, the writer of this scripture is talking about Christian brothers.

On August 20, 2015, I found out how blessed I am with great friends, especially during times of trouble. On that day, my dog, who would have been 14-years-old that year, became unexpectedly ill. Since it was after hours for my regular veterinarian, I had to rush my beloved pet to an emergency clinic about 30 miles away.

A neighbor, also a wonderful friend, agreed to accompany me that evening. She had already prepared herself for bed but hurriedly donned her clothes and was on my front door step in less than 10 minutes.

Like me, Sonya loves all of God's creatures. So when I was told my beloved pet had to be euthanized or he would continue to suffer, I was devastated. I burst into tears. So did my friend as we held each other and sobbed.

After sharing my loss on social media, I was amazed at the comments and feedback I received from friends, former students and people whom I have never met. Prayers and encouragement were offered. I received more than 200 condolences, including phone calls to check on me.

The next day, another dear friend took me to lunch. She handed me a card, one she obviously had to stop and purchase before she met me. She listened as I poured out my heart about the pet I had owned since he was eight weeks old. We cried. We laughed. That's what friends do.

Another friend has called several times to check on me. He always called Taco, "his little buddy."

Two days later, another friend called to offer condolences. We spoke for over 30 minutes and he said something I didn't think I was prepared to do. He encouraged me to adopt another dog.

While I had planned to wait, he said, "Carol, you have so much love to give. You poured it out on Taco and he loved you back. He would want you to be happy. Just think, you can sit with that new puppy on your lap and tell her about Taco."

I smiled upon hearing his words. Friendships are precious. The issue here is that in order to have a friend, one must be a friend.

One of the best friends we can ever have is Jesus. He will never leave us nor forsake us. Are you that kind of friend?

Follow Through

Eliminate: It's difficult sometimes to sever ties with those who hinder you from being your best for the Lord. While I've had to do that at times, I'm still blessed with many people who care about me. I discovered this when my precious dog died. I've learned to treasure my best friends and accept the friendship offered by those who aren't as close. Have you had to sever ties with those you once thought were your friends? What happened? Looking back, do you think it was the best choice for you? Why or why not?

Enlist: Reread the definition of a friend on page 102. Do you have at least one friend that fits this description? How did you meet? How long have you been friends? If you have more than one friend who meets these criteria, you are truly blessed. Let them know what their friendship means to you by writing a letter or sending a card to each one.

Enrich: Seek ways to encourage and enhance the friendships you already have. Become the kind of friend as described in the definition on page 102. Make a list of ways you are already that kind of friend. Make a list of those things you could do to strengthen your friendship.

WEEK 32

THE GIFT OF FRIENDSHIP

"The righteous choose their friends carefully, but the way of the wicked leads them astray"—Proverbs 12:26 (NIV).

Can you recall your first best friend? I can. Her name is Gwen.

I've not seen nor talked to Gwen in more than 45 years, but I still remember her. Several months before my 16th birthday, my family relocated from Louisiana to Oklahoma, where my parents grew up.

At first, I stayed in touch via snail mail. In the late 60s, hand-written letters were the common form of long-distance communication. Email and texting weren't a daily staple of our lives.

Times have changed but not our need for friendships. Each new chapter in my life has included new friends. As the pages turn, my life is enriched by this circle of friends.

When I was diagnosed with breast cancer in 2002, one friend showed up on my doorstep with a white rose of hope. Other friends drove me to pre- and post-op doctor visits.

While visiting with a friend over lunch one day, I laughed when she crumbled her chips into her tortilla soup. Because my friend teaches etiquette classes, I found it humorous when she explained that you really shouldn't do that in public. However, since we are friends, she felt comfortable enough to ignore that tip.

Friends come in all shapes and sizes. Some offer their big heart. Others offer a shoulder on which to cry. Some bring sunshine and some listen to you whine. Others will speak the truth, even when it hurts. Pals will compliment us, hug us, send birthday cards, and encourage us to keep putting one foot in front of the other when we want to give up. Yet, we may only hear once a year from another friend.

I receive a Christmas card each December from my college roommate. We rarely talk on the phone. Occasionally, we e-mail each other, but each time we communicate, it seems as if it has been only a day or two since we last visited. Our relationship has lasted for more than 40 years.

Renewing old friendships that have ended on a less-than-pleasant note is also heart-warming. Several months ago, I had a dream about a friend with whom I had not spoken in almost two years. Our relationship had become strained due to circumstances at work. When I retired and moved to a new community, we lost touch. After my dream, I felt led by God to contact her. I picked up the phone one evening and said, "Judy, this is Carol. How are you doing?"

Our long-distance conversation was a time for catching up on each other's lives and a time for healing. Before she hung up the phone, she said, "Carol, I think of you often and I just want to say, 'I love you.'"

One thing we should never ignore is our need for friends. We were created for relationships. When those relationships enhance our life and help us to grow into the person God created us to be, then we can be assured it is truly His gift.

Follow Through

Eliminate: Is there a friend from your past whom you have not spoken to in a long time? Did your friendship end on a sour note? Was there a disagreement? What caused the rift? How do you feel about that friend today?

Enlist: If you have parted ways with a friend and no longer communicate with her, pray about the relationship, especially if God has placed that person on your heart. Do you feel led to contact her? What is the best way to approach this friend? E-mail? Phone? A hand-written note?

Enrich: Write a letter of encouragement to a close friend who is going through a difficult time. What can you say to help her cope during this time? Pray for God to give you the right words for the situation.

WEEK 33

WHEN YOU GIVE YOURSELF AWAY

"But whatever is good and perfect comes to us from God, the Creator of all light, and he shines forever without change or shadow"—James 1:17 (TLB).

Climbing on a small step ladder, I reached the top corner shelf in my kitchen. I stretched toward the back to retrieve the crystal décor and glassware that had been a part of my mother's collection. My sister and I had split the set after our father passed in 2007. Our mother had gone to be with the Lord in 2004.

The pieces in question had been in the same place since I'd brought them home. As I moved them carefully onto the countertop, I wondered why I'd kept them. I'm not sentimental about things, especially those taking up space, requiring maintenance or providing no value to my life.

While some might criticize me for my lack of sentimentality, I confess I've kept a few things belonging to my parents and grandparents—usually those with a background story. However, the crystal décor was rarely used. It was simply that—décor. The glassware was only used on special occasions, like holidays.

When I contacted my sister and offered her the pieces, she was more than happy to take them off my hands. That meant less packing for me as I prepared to move once again. They are also items my sister will probably use.

While there's nothing wrong with having beautiful things, they can—if we allow them—get in the way of what God has planned for us. Luke tells us in Chapter 9 that when Jesus sent His disciples out to proclaim the kingdom of God, He said, *"Take nothing for the journey—no staff, no bag, no bread, no money, no extra shirt."*

Not only was Jesus teaching them to rely on God for their provision,

He was warning them about seeking praise from others based on their outward appearance. Jesus wanted the message to be heard without distraction.

Anything can become a distraction if it takes the place of God in our lives. Matthew tells us in Chapter 6:19-21, *"Do not lay up for yourselves treasures on earth, where moth and rust destroy and where thieves break in and steal, but lay up for yourselves treasures in heaven, where neither moth nor rust destroys and where thieves do not break in and steal. For where your treasure is, there your heart will be also."*

My heart belongs to Jesus. Therefore, I've found myself giving away many treasured items to friends. I knew I would not miss those things; however, I knew I would miss the many friends I had made while living there. I was starting a new chapter in my life.

I enjoyed giving away clothing, jewelry and other accessories as well as décor, books and mementos. When I offered an antique tray to a friend who had admired it, she said, "But that belonged to your grandmother. You can't give it away."

Yes it did, but because my friend has done so much for me, I wanted to bless her. I have my memories.

Follow Through

Eliminate: Is it time to eliminate things in your life that no longer contribute in any way to your joy or hinder your relationship with the Lord or takes time away from your relationships? Look around your house and see what you can give away. Do you have a friend or friends who might appreciate the items you want to get rid of to downsize? Give them away.

Enlist: Do you have a special friend in your life that you have lost track of since you've relocated or changed jobs? Do you find yourself thinking of that friend, wishing you could see her again? When you can, reconnect with her through social media, a phone call or a letter. If the time is available and the distance is not too far, make time to have lunch with her?

Enrich: In Matthew, Jesus tells us not to store up treasures on earth. However, we should treasure our friends. How would everyone's life change if we chose friends over things? What would our society look like if people were more important to us than the things we own?

In your journal, ask yourself, "Do I treasure things over people?" Honestly examine your life for an indication of your priorities. Ask the Holy Spirit to reveal the answer if you are not certain.

WEEK 34

ALL THE DAYS OF OUR LIVES

"Surely goodness and mercy shall follow me all the days of my life and I will dwell in the house of the Lord forever—Psalm 23:6 (KJV).

I am grateful for so many things. I'm grateful for the wonderful people whom the Lord has brought into my life, especially over the last 20 years.

I'm also grateful for the doors of opportunity He has opened for me to share my writing with others. His hand guides mine as I touch the keys of my computer.

I'm grateful for my health, my sons, my grandchildren and my church family. I'm grateful that I am in good health and that I have a roof over my head. I am also grateful my 15-year-old automobile ran well, until it hit almost 180,000 miles in 2016 and started giving me trouble. I'm thankful I could afford a newer, reliable replacement. If I continued with my gratitude list, I'd never finish this book.

I recall an email I received from a friend one day, just when I needed it. It was a sunny day and she commented: "Isn't the sunshine beautiful? I was just thinking how blessed we are."

She commented on the people from all walks of life she had talked to that day. But what she had felt all day was the presence that connects us all—the hope everlasting.

"Just as we know the sunshine will always follow a storm, so is our assurance that goodness and mercy will follow us all the days of our lives," she wrote.

Her email lifted me up that day. Even though I seek Him every morning through Bible study and prayer, it is refreshing to hear another believer's testimony. Many times, we forget that even believers need encouragement and reminders of God's goodness. We can get discouraged in a world whose values are wrapped up in material things.

God's goodness and mercy is available to all. As believers, we reach out to those who are hurting—those who need to know about God's love and forgiveness, His kindness and patience.

As I was writing this devotion late one Saturday evening, I reached a roadblock or as wordsmiths say—a writer's block. All writers, at one time or another, experience the fear of not having the words to finish a piece.

I tried and tried late that night to finish this piece. I struggled with where God was leading me. I finally quit struggling and went to bed, content that God would bring the inspiration I needed to finish this piece.

The next morning in church, He did. Our pastor's sermon was God's answer that He would help me finish this devotional. One statement that Pastor Ray made was, "Sometimes we need encouragement when we have doubts and we wonder if we can go on."

He talked about the people who have the gift of encouragement. I have been told it is one of my gifts. However, I've discovered that even encouragers need encouragement sometimes. This finished devotional is proof of that.

We serve an awesome God. His mercy and goodness follow us all the days of our lives.

Follow Through

Eliminate: When we eliminate the negativity from our lives by being grateful for what we have, we are open to more of God's blessings. I've discovered that my friends are a big source of those blessings. Recall a time when you experienced God's blessings through a friend. What happened? When you think about that time, how do you feel now?

Enlist: Make a list of your blessings each day. On that list, include the names of friends whose friendship you treasure and why.

Enrich: Think of ways to be a blessing to others. Sometimes we take our close friends for granted. How can you express your appreciation to those special friends? Make a list and follow through.

WEEK 35

HOW ARE YOU SPENDING YOUR DAYS?

"Teach us to number our days and recognize how few they are; help us to spend them as we should"—Psalm 90:12 (TLB).

With each passing year, I become more aware of the brevity of life. In 2016, I celebrated my 63rd birthday. When a friend phoned to wish me a happy birthday, we discussed how long we'd known each other.

We were surprised when we realized it had been more than a decade. Our friendship has grown during that time, making me realize the necessity of having and nurturing those relationships that are important to making life worthwhile.

A recent post on Facebook made me think about the importance of relationships vs. things. Things don't bring happiness. Both are fleeting. However, we were made for a relationship with each other.

The post follows: "I believe as we grow older our Christmas list gets smaller and the things we really want for the holidays can't be bought."

What is more important than to be surrounded by family and friends who love us in spite of our faults and failures? Nothing in my book! No gift can replace the shared laughter, the tears, the disagreements, the heartache, the pain or the victories. Nothing! Money cannot buy the experiences we share.

Money also can't purchase the kind of friend who won't agree with you to make you happy. Instead, the best of friends will say what needs to be said, whether you want to hear it or not. I have several friends like that. Whether I complain or am feeling sorry for myself, none of these three let me stew in my pity very long. They love me enough to encourage me with kind but honest words.

How we spend our days is important in God's kingdom. We can spend our days in pursuit of money to purchase material things for our own gratification, or we can spend our days pursuing what really matters.

Romans 14:19 says, *"So then we pursue the things which make for peace and the building up of one another."*

A proclaimed agnostic and prominent trial lawyer, Clarence Darrow had this to say about the brevity of life. "When we fully understand the brevity of life, its fleeting joys and unavoidable pains; when we accept the facts that all men and women are approaching an inevitable doom: the consciousness of it should make us more kindly and considerate of each other. This feeling should make men and women use their best efforts to help their fellow travelers on the road, to make the path brighter and easier as we journey on. It should bring a closer kinship, a better understanding, and a deeper sympathy for the wayfarers who must live a common life and die a common death."

However, life isn't common when we live each day for Jesus. Our lives can be extraordinary when we follow in His steps. When the Gospel becomes the defining reality of our lives, we begin to look at every-thing differently.

Only then will our days really count.

Follow Through

Eliminate: The statement in paragraph four says, "As we grow older our Christmas gift list gets smaller and the things we really want for the holidays can't be bought." Do you agree with this statement? Why or why not? Reflect in your journal on the importance of friendships vs. owning stuff.

Enlist: Do you have a small circle of friends who keep you accountable? For example, if you're having a pity party, do they offer sympathy and encouragement to help you move forward during difficult times?

Enrich: Friends enrich our lives, especially those girlfriends who know our deepest secrets but love us anyway. Do you make it a habit of spending time with them or are they an afterthought when you do find some spare time? Make time for a regular girls' luncheon or other outing to help your friendships thrive. Reread Romans 14:19 on the previous page and reflect in your journal about the meaning for you. What are you pursuing?

September

Heal, Honor, Hope

"but those who hope in the LORD will renew their strength. They will soar on wings like eagles; they will run and not grow weary, they will walk and not be faint"— Isaiah 40:31(NIV).

Like the frogs plaguing the Egyptians and making them miserable, there can be things in our lives, like self-pity, anger, bitterness, depression and unforgiveness that we tote around with us every day. Carrying this load can leave us hopeless and prone to disease.

Maybe you weren't popular in school. Maybe you weren't a star athlete or the homecoming queen. Maybe you come from a broken home or you were abused, verbally, physically or sexually. Maybe you've been betrayed by family or friends, leaving you brokenhearted and distrustful. I've been there. Maybe you have too.

Sometimes, the betrayal is not obvious but happens over a period of time. In her book titled, *Daring Greatly: How The Courage To Be Vulnerable Transforms The Way We Live, Love, Parent, and Lead*, author Brené Brown, writes: "When the people we love or with whom we have a deep connection stop caring, stop paying attention, stop investing and fighting for the relationship, trust begins to slip away and hurt starts seeping in. Disengagement triggers shame and our greatest fears—the fears of being abandoned, unworthy, and unlovable."

However, we don't have to wallow in self-pity or sink into a depression. Our Heavenly Father welcomes us with open arms. He will never leave us or forsake us.

Psalm 34:18-19 says, *"The Lord is close to the brokenhearted; He rescues those who are crushed in spirit. The righteous face many troubles, but the Lord rescues them from each and every one."*

In September, we will examine our past, but not wallow in it. Why is it important to do so? I've learned that unless we deal with the past and unpack our baggage, we can't be all God has created us to be.

Until I dealt with my insecurities and my pain from "not fitting in," I couldn't move forward. Isaiah 43:18-19 says,

> *"Forget the former things;*
> *do not dwell on the past.*
> *See, I am doing a new thing!*
> *Now it springs up; do you not perceive it?*
> *I am making a way in the wilderness*
> *and streams in the wasteland."*

WEEK 36

JUST LET IT GO

"Anyone who belongs to Christ is a new person. The past is forgotten, and everything is new"— *2 Corinthians 5:17 (CEV).*

Although I've not seen it, I've heard the lyrics to the song associated with Disney's popular animated movie, "Frozen." Sung by little girls who have seen the film, the song's title is "Let it Go."

I looked up the lyrics to the catchy tune. When I read them, I thought, "How appropriate for anyone who wants to let go of the past and embrace the new?"

Recently, I was having lunch with a couple of friends. As usual, we shared several belly laughs when we revealed some of our deepest desires and thoughts—just girl talk. While I can't recall how the subject led to our past, I found myself confessing some of the more "ornery" things I'd done when I was younger.

Since my friends have only known the person I am now, they were surprised by my confessions. While those escapades weren't necessarily earth-shattering, they were definitely a part of the person I was before Jesus got ahold of me.

When we belong to Him, we become a new creation. He forgets our past. Everything becomes new. Even the Old Testament reminds us in Isaiah 43:18 to *"Forget the former things; do not dwell on the past (NIV).*

Each morning is a good time to examine our lives and let go of those things holding us back from spiritual growth. Growing spiritually requires us to be intentional.

I came across the following suggestions in an article titled "Seven Steps to Letting Go of the Past" by Susan Gregory and thought it appropriate.

First, let go of the baggage from your past. Clinging to anything from your former life keeps you from God's best (See Jeremiah 29:11). Gregory suggests making a list of past pains and then burning the paper in a "ceremonial" fire.

Second, close that chapter on your life. Like a book we've just finished, it's time to turn the page on a new one (See Isaiah 43:18 on the previous page). Remember, that was then, this is now.

Third, quit talking about your past. That's difficult when you're still clinging to heavy baggage (See Proverbs 18:21).

Fourth, let go of the shame, another difficult step for some of us. However, we all make mistakes. Consciously or unconsciously, we hurt others as well as ourselves in the process. "Thankfully," says Gregory, "we have Jesus!" (See 1 John 1:9).

Fifth, enjoy today. We can't change the past. No one can. However, we can be grateful for each new day we are given (See Psalm 118:24).

Sixth, walk by faith and not by sight. How can you do that? Focus on God's Word instead of your circumstances. If you don't already read and study the Bible every day, begin now (See Joshua 1:8).

Seventh, believe and understand the power of forgiveness. Refusing to forgive someone doesn't hurt the other person. It only hurts you (See Matthew 6:14-15).

Isn't it time to just "let it go?"

Follow Through

Heal: What from your past do you need to confess? If it is too painful or embarrassing to share with a friend or your pastor, write a letter to Jesus in your journal. If it is something painful, ask Him to help you let it go. If it is embarrassing, ask Him to help you understand that it no longer matters.

Honor: Reread the list of suggestions in the article by Susan Gregory. Reflect on the steps, writing down anything that comes to mind in your journal. What baggage do you need to let go of to move into the future God has for you?

Hope: Look back at your thoughts from the previous exercise. What steps do you need to take to go from hopeless to hopeful? Start with the first step and follow through. Ask Jesus to help you with each step of your journey as you turn to a new chapter in your life.

(NOTE: If you have suffered severe trauma, like physical, sexual or verbal abuse, seek a qualified counselor if you have not already done so.)

WEEK 37

IT ISN'T A GIFT UNTIL YOU GIVE IT AWAY

"We have different gifts, according to the grace given us"—
Romans 12:6 (NIV).

When I was in elementary school—way back when—I dreaded math. I was not good at it.

Oh, I could do simple arithmetic, but when the problem became too complicated, forget it. That's why I would sit terrified that the teacher would call on me to go to the chalkboard and solve an equation before the class.

When I was in the fourth grade—that would have been in the 60s—the race was on to beat the Russians to the moon. This led to the teaching of "new math" or "space math" in many American schools.

I didn't care what they called it; it was still "way out there" for my math-impaired mind. My creative mind refuses to function with a formula.

While some people get high on solving algebraic equations, I can break out in hives if I am even exposed to a mathematics problem.

A teaching friend of mine is an example of one who gets so excited when she is challenged with any type of mathematics problem that she almost bursts into a song and dance routine. One day we were discussing the benefits of being required to take college algebra.

Being mathematically-challenged, I could see no earthly reason why I, or anyone else who is handicapped like myself, should have to suffer through another semester of any type of math after graduation from high school.

It had been over 30 years since I had been forced to take college algebra. I told my friend, "If you placed an algebra test before me right now, held a gun to my head and told me I had to pass the test, I'd have to say, 'Just shoot me now because I can't pass it.'"

My strengths are in reading and writing. I have loved the written word since I learned to read "See Dick and Jane." Give me a napkin and a writing utensil and I can fill the space with more than just directions. I love words.

According to my parents, my creative mind is not the only gift that God has given me.

When I was a child, my mother would grow tired of my incessant chattering. She would ask, "Carol, don't your jaws ever get tired?"

Innocently, I'd answer, "No mama," to which she would reply, "Well, my ears sure do."

My Dad always said I was vaccinated with a Victrola needle when I was born. If you don't know what that is, it was one of the first phonograph machines or an early record player manufactured in the early 1900s.

Until I read a chapter on applying your abilities in *The Purpose Driven Life*, I thought my motor mouth was a curse. In the book, Pastor Rick Warren says, "Your abilities are the natural talents you were born with. Some people have a natural ability with words: They came out of the womb talking!"

I confess. That's me.

We're all blessed with different gifts. As Pastor Warren says, "It would be a boring world if we were all plain vanilla."

Are you using your gifts to glorify God? A gift isn't a gift until you give it away.

Follow Through

Heal: Is there an area of your life where you feel insufficient? In what way have you underestimated yourself? If you are uncertain, ask someone close to help you evaluate your strengths and weaknesses.

Honor: Although math was never my strength, I can now joke about my lack of talent in that area. I'm just happy that 95 percent of the time, I can balance my checkbook. What special gift do you bring to the world? How can you use it to help others?

Hope: If you simply followed your heart, what actions would you take? If you've discovered your God-given talents, what will enable you to take the next important step to further develop that gift? Who can help you reach your goals? Who can you help on her journey to discovering and using her gifts for His kingdom work?

WEEK 38

WITH JESUS BY YOUR SIDE

"Yours, O Lord, are the greatness, the power, the glory, the victory, and the majesty; for all that is in the heavens and on the earth is yours; yours is the kingdom, O Lord, and you are exalted as head above all"
—1 Chronicles 29:11(NRSV).

More than once I've said to friends, "I don't know how people make it through life without Jesus."

Since rededicating my life to Him 16 years ago, I've had my share of trouble. While having Jesus in your life doesn't exclude you from trials, you can bet He's by your side when those times come. And they will come in the form of financial, physical, emotional and relational struggles.

Evangelist Billy Graham once said, "Even the securest financial plan and the finest health coverage aren't enough to hold us steady when the challenges come. We need something more, something deeper and unshakeable, something that will see us through life's hard times."

Before I had a personal relationship with my Savior and Lord, trials would send me into a tailspin. I'd rant, and then panic, before trying to find a solution. That's because I was relying on myself. I thought I had to solve everything on my own. My pride wouldn't let me admit I couldn't fix everything and everyone. It just doesn't work.

What does work is submitting ourselves to Jesus. While we can wrestle for control, ultimately, we're not in charge. We only think we are.

In a recent *Mornings with Jesus* devotional, author Susanna Foth Aughtmon, wrote, "Lately, I've been trying to be the lord of my life. And I have this picture in my mind of Jesus sitting back on His heels taking in my chaos and my sorry attempts at controlling my circumstances and my astounding lack of resources and saying, 'So how is that working for you?' Of course, He knows it is absolutely not working for me and mostly, I am a wreck. So today I am trying something different. I am going to let Him be Lord. Because…He is, I know it will make a difference."

Although it has taken me many years to acknowledge God's sovereignty, I'm glad I did. Since then, I've learned He is in control. He is the One who opens doors. He is the One who always makes a way. He is the One who provides healing. He is the One who brings peace— a peace that only comes when you surrender to Him.

In Matthew 11:28-30, Jesus says, *"Come to me and I will give you rest—all of you who work so hard beneath a heavy yoke. Wear my yoke—for it fits perfectly—and let me teach you; for I am gentle and humble, and you shall find rest for your souls; for I give you only light burdens."*

If you don't already start your day with Jesus, spend some time with Him in prayer. Then, invite Him to be in charge of your life. During the day, seek His guidance when you have a decision to make.

Follow Through

Heal: Have trials left you drained, wondering if God has forsaken you? More than once in scripture God has told His children, "I will never leave you nor forsake you." Locate all of the scriptures in both the Old and New Testaments referencing this promise from our Heavenly Father. Write them in your journal. Meditate on this promise. Journal a letter to God, thanking Him for all the trials He has seen you through.

Honor: Have you surrendered your will to His? Why or why not? What do you think that means? Can you think of times in your life when you didn't? What happened? Can you remember times when you did submit your will to Him? How did things turn out? Which is easier for you? Why?

Hope: Psalm 37:7 says, *"Surrender yourself to the Lord, and wait patiently for him."* Patience is a virtue and something we acquire as we spend more time in His Word. How can being patient bring hope in times of trouble? What does hope look like to you? Journal your answers.

WEEK 39

WHEN WILL YOU BE GOOD ENOUGH FOR LOVE?

"But God showed his great love for us by sending Christ to die for us while we were still sinners"— Romans 5:8 (NLT).

Growing up, I never felt as if I were good enough. My mother expected perfection from her daughters. In retrospect, I'm sure she followed in the footsteps of her own mother. Both meant well.

When you're raised to seek perfection, you never feel worthy. A feeling of unworthiness leads to insecurity in all your relationships. Striving to earn the love of others leads to internal conflict. Being a people pleaser creates a false identity.

Until I came to know Jesus as my redeemer and Lord, I never understood the meaning of "unconditional" love. I struggled, like others, to understand how God could love me without any conditions attached.

Pastor Charles Stanley says, ". . . maybe we just feel unworthy of His love. Well, I have news for you: No one is worthy. God's love is based not on whether we are deserving but on His character—we need to understand that love isn't simply something God does; it's who He is."

In 1 John 4:8, the writer penned, *"But anyone who does not love does not know God, for God is love."*

As I've grown in my faith, I've found security in the arms of a Heavenly Father who will never leave me nor forsake me. I embrace His love for me, but still struggle with the bloody sacrifice of His Son on the cross. He did that for me? Yes, but His plan included all of mankind.

It's easier to understand unconditional love when you become a parent. British journalist Tony Parsons wrote, "When he was born, I looked at my little boy and felt an unconditional love I never knew was inside me. As he grew, and I watched him stagger about, speak his first words, and turn into a beautiful little boy, that feeling did not change."

God is like that, too. However, He knew us before we were ever born. He formed us in our mother's womb. He loves us unconditionally. Those feelings never change. His story is our story.

Some go to extremes to achieve acceptance in His eyes, but fail dismally. Then, they find His love and grace transcend their failures. His mercies are new each morning.

In Kay Bruner's memoir, *As Soon as I Fell*, she shares her family's story of going to extremes for spiritual acceptability. With a marriage and ministry built on high performance and spiritual heroism, the couple eventually experienced burnout and depression. A radical reinvention of their life, now based on a nourishing intimate connection with God, led to their understanding of unconditional love. You can't earn it. You can't buy it. However, you can find hope and healing in His love.

When will you be good enough for love? Gaze upon the cross. Look at the outstretched arms of your Savior. Embrace the love of a Heavenly Father who loves His children so much He gave His one and only Son that we might have life everlasting.

Follow Through

Heal: Perfectionism means that one sets standards so high they either cannot be met, or are only met with great difficulty. A perfectionist believes that anything short of perfection is unacceptable and that even minor imperfections will lead to a disaster. Does that describe you? It did me.

But being a perfectionist sets one up for failure. We can never be perfect nor can we achieve perfection. That's why Jesus is the only answer to our imperfections. Ask yourself the following questions to determine if you are a perfectionist:

1. Do you have trouble meeting your own standards?
2. Do you often feel frustrated, depressed, anxious or angry while trying to meet your standards?
3. Has anyone ever told you that your standards are too high?
4. Do your standards get in the way? For example, do they make it difficult for you to meet deadlines, finish a task, trust others or do anything spontaneously?

If you answered "yes" to any of the above questions, you may be struggling with perfectionism.

Honor: If you constantly criticize yourself, feel depressed, frustrated, anxious, or even angry, it's time to let it go with God's help. Write the following scriptures down on 3 x 5 index cards. Post them around your house or carry them with you in your purse as a reminder to put your life in His hands.

1. Matthew 11:28-30
2. Luke 10:41-42
3. John 8:10-11
4. 2 Corinthians 12:9
5. Hebrews 4:15-16

Hope: Realize you will never be perfect and neither will any area of your life. Remember: life is about God—the only perfect One. When you find yourself making a project more important than your Heavenly Father's desire for your life, ask yourself, "Am I viewing this project through the lens of faith or through the eyes of culture? If you're doing the latter, you may be hurting others in your quest for perfection. You don't have to earn God's love.

Can you recall a time when you made a project more important than God's desires for your life? What happened? What would you tell God about this now? Have you asked for His forgiveness and direction?

October

Trust, Thrive, Treasure

"May the God of hope fill you with all joy and peace as you trust in him, so that you may overflow with hope by the power of the Holy Spirit"— Romans 15:13 (NIV).

Trust is a valuable character trait often lacking in today's world. Learning to trust God in every circumstance and in every area of our lives requires us to seek Him daily for our needs and to thank Him for what He has already done for us.

What does it mean to trust in God? To trust is to place your full confidence in Who He is.

In today's world, we're constantly exposed to our culture through 24/7 social media as well as television. Our culture tries to dictate what is acceptable in man's eyes. For example, we're bombarded with news reports of Hollywood and sports celebrities whose choices don't line up with God's Word.

I'm always amazed—and a tad irritated—when a news anchor says something similar to the following: "Everyone is waiting anxiously for the announcement about celebrity so-and-so (*insert famous name here*) and her celebrity boyfriend (*insert famous name here*) who are expecting their first child together. We've heard rumors they're going to name their baby, a boy, such-and such (*insert unusual baby name here*)."

You're kidding me. Right? I'm not everyone. I really don't care about an unmarried celebrity couple having a child. Yet stories like this grab nightly news headlines on a regular basis. I realize that having a child out-of-wedlock is culturally acceptable today. But the media hype makes it even more acceptable.

If we put out trust in anyone or anything other than the God of the universe, what does that say about our Christian walk? If we find cultural trends acceptable, have we forsaken our first love, Jesus Christ?

To survive today's cultural onslaught and thrive in our walk with the Lord, we must be intentional about our spiritual growth. To treasure the Holy Word, we must spend time reading and studying scripture.

In October, our focus will be on learning to trust God more, thriving in our walk with Jesus and treasuring those moments when His Word reveals a spiritual nugget of truth, bringing peace and hope in this fallen world.

WEEK 40

SEVEN DAILY STEPS TO TRUSTING GOD

"Trust in the Lord with all your heart; do not depend on your own understanding. Seek his will in all you do, and he will show you which path to take."— Proverbs 3:5-6(NLT).

Proverbs 3:5-6 is one of my favorite scriptures. I've posted it on my computer monitor. I have it memorized as a daily reminder. As I've grown spiritually, letting go of the need to be in control, I've learned to lean on God.

In a "Bible Study Tools" article by John Upchurch, he gives readers seven daily steps to trusting God with all your heart. Following this advice each day will enable you to have a greater trust in where God is leading you and why.

1. *Don't depend on you.* "We live in a world where trust must be earned and seems to be in short supply," says the author. But wise King Solomon, who wrote Proverbs, knew that trust is where we must start (see Proverbs 3:5). Disappointments teach us to depend upon ourselves. However, "living the life God has called us to means unlearning that lesson—to rest in God's understanding" and not our own." But, what if we don't feel like we can trust Him completely? The author says, "That's where step two comes in."

2. *Cry out to God.* "Surrendering to God begins with our lips and our thoughts," the author adds. We need to cry out to Him to show we depend on Him (See Proverbs 3:6). When we pray, we're confessing His ways are better. When we surrender our lives to Him, we have to remember step three.

3. *Run from evil.* "So much in our world can clutter our relationship with God," the author says. In 1 John 2:16, the writer describes "them as the desires of the flesh, the lusts of the eyes and the pride in our lives." They become stumbling

blocks when we think we deserve them to be happy. Instead, life works best when we remember God is the source of our blessings.

4. *Put God first in your life.* We're selfish beings; even so, when we put God first, trusting everything we own to His keeping, including our money, we're admitting how much we depend on Him.

5. *Check yourself by God's Word.* We're not so good at evaluating ourselves. I know I'm not. We make excuses for our behavior. If we are to truly trust God, we need to know where we stand by studying His Truth.

6. *Listen to the Holy Spirit.* As we go through our day, the Holy Spirit guides us. That means we're never alone if we will listen (John 14:26).

7. *Rest in God's Love.* Living in a difficult world often makes us wonder if God even cares. You might ask, "Where is God when I need Him?" Solomon reminds us God never leaves us to fend for ourselves.

Even in the midst of turmoil, God is with us, using our challenges to teach us how to trust in Him with all our hearts. It takes whole-hearted commitment each day but we're never alone (Matthew 28:20b).

Follow Through

Trust: Have you learned to trust God? Why or why not? Give an example of a time when you didn't and what happened. Can you recall a time when you did trust Him for the outcome of something? What happened?

Thrive: To thrive, according to dictionary.com means several things: "to prosper; be fortunate or successful. And to grow or develop vigorously; flourish." Are you thriving on God's presence or are you afraid to let go and trust Him? Why or why not?

Treasure: One way to treasure God's Word is to spend time reading and meditating on scripture each morning before your day gets busy. Keep your journal nearby to jot down those scriptures that speak to you and why. As you make time for God's Word, you'll be surprised at the treasures you'll discover.

Do you have a special scripture or scriptures that encourage you? What are they? How do they encourage you?

WEEK 41

WHAT DOES HOPE DO FOR MANKIND?

"But in your hearts revere Christ as Lord. Always be prepared to give an answer to everyone who asks you to give the reason for the hope that you have"—1 Peter 3:15 (NIV).

The three of us clasped hands and bowed our heads. We were standing in the middle of a discount department store aisle, praying for an employee who was battling brain cancer. Covering the lower half of her face was a protective mask to ward off the threat of germs.

My friend, Sonya, knew the employee and introduced us. As the woman's story unfolded, I learned it wasn't her first battle with cancer. Her fighting spirit drew me in as did her positive attitude.

As we continued shopping, we struck up a conversation with another store employee who had beat cancer. She shared her amazing story of healing. Placed on hospice, her only hope was divine intervention. Prayers were answered and this amazing woman is, indeed, a walking miracle.

Both women have placed their hope in God. Hope. What does it look like? For me, hope shines brightest when I'm at my lowest.

Hope is the word I recently chose to study in the scriptures. Each morning, after I read my daily devotional, I turn to the concordance in the back of my *Women of Faith Bible* and look up verses referencing hope. One of my favorites is Jeremiah 29:11: *"For I know the plans I have for you," declares the Lord, "plans to prosper you and not to harm you, plans to give you hope and a future."*

The word "prosper" jumps out at us. Immediately, we think of material riches. But this verse is often taken out of context.

Author Mary DeMuth, addressing this misunderstanding, explains. "The heart of the verse is 'not that we would escape our lot, but that we would learn to thrive' in the midst of it."

However, to understand, we need the back story. In exile, the Israelites were being punished by God as result of their disobedience. Jeremiah, the prophet, confronts Hananiah, the false prophet, for boldly proclaiming that God was going to free Israel from Babylon in two years. Confronting Hananiah's lie, Jeremiah states the promise we read in this verse. God did indeed have a good plan for the fickle Israelites.

However, Jeremiah's message from God in the seventh verse says, *"seek the peace and the prosperity of the city to which I have carried you into exile. Pray to the Lord for it, because if it prospers, you too will prosper."*

Was this the message the Israelites wanted to hear? Hardly! Then, God hits them with a bigger blow. In verse 10, He reveals His promise will be fulfilled after 70 years. The current generation would never return to their home.

DeMuth writes, "...let's remember that the best growth comes through persevering through trials, not escaping them entirely."

Cling to the truth where you will find hope in the midst of trials. Hope. You can't bottle it. You can't buy it. However, you can share it.

Follow Through

Trust: When life is going well, it's easy to feel hopeful. But when trouble comes our way in the form of a serious illness, financial issues, or the loss of a loved one, feelings of hopelessness can overwhelm us. Reread the devotional above. What do you think kept these two women going in the face of adversity? I believe it was hope. Only God can offer us more than just a feeling. When we have a deep, abiding relationship with our Heavenly Father, His presence is always with us. Evaluate your relationship with our Abba Father. Are you as close to Him as you'd like to be? Why or why not? Journal your thought about this heavenly relationship. What spiritual disciplines could help you to draw closer to Him?

Thrive: Are you thriving in hope? What does that mean to you? To me, it means that no matter what happens in my life, I can trust God to see me through. My hope is in Him. My future is in His hands. Have you experienced that hope? When? Share that experience as a testimony with another person who may need encouragement. Write that experience down in your journal as a reminder of God's work in your life.

Treasure: Even when times are tough, you can do much more than endure the situation. You can actually enjoy life to the fullest—even in the middle of the worst circumstances. Remember that life is a gift from God. Embrace it! When you do, you will notice His presence with you and rejoice when you sense Him nearby. Treasure those moments and ask the Holy Spirit to renew your mind each day. With a positive attitude, you will thrive no matter what is going on in your life.

Look up the following scriptures and write them in your journal as a reminder of God's presence in your life:

- Genesis 28:16
- Exodus 33:14
- Deuteronomy 4:29
- Psalms 16:11
- Psalms 34:18-19
- Psalms 46:1
- Psalms 145:18-19
- Proverbs 15:3
- Isaiah 55:6
- 1 Thessalonians 2:19
- Hebrews 13:5-6
- James 4:8

If it will encourage you, write one or more of these scriptures on index cards and post them around the house as a reminder of His presence.

WEEK 42

ARE YOU DOING LIFE GOD'S WAY?

"Now faith is confidence in what we hope for and assurance about what we do not see"— Hebrews 11:1 (CEB).

The lyrics to an old Frank Sinatra tune come back to haunt me sometimes. Part of the song goes, "I planned each charted course, each careful step along the byway and more, much more than this, I did it my way."

Why do these words resonate with me? Before Jesus got ahold of me, I tried to chart my own course. I tried to do things my way. Looking back, I can see my way wasn't always the best. I didn't consult the Maker of the Universe before making a decision, especially those affecting not only me, but others as well.

My confidence was in my own ability to get things done. My faith and hope and assurance rested solely on what I could perceive with my own eyes. I resisted change unless I was in control.

In 2001, a life-changing experience opened my eyes and I began seeking God. As I have grown to trust Him more, my confidence now lies solely in Him. Do I still I have doubts sometimes? Yes. Do I still question God? Yes.

However, if I hadn't taken a leap of faith and trusted Him to catch me if I failed, I wouldn't be on the path that has led to my current writing and speaking ministry. If I hadn't trusted God, I would never have left the comfort of family and friends and moved to another community in 2005. That move led to more adventures, including mission trips overseas and a trip to the Holy Land.

Being obedient and open to change has led me to move several times. Just about the time I get comfortable, God opens another door. In the past, I would have dug my heels in and refused. Even though God gives us free will, I want to do life His way.

Without being open to change and doing life God's way, we miss out on opportunities we never dreamed we would have. Is it always easy? No. I continually remind myself He will never lead me astray.

Below are 10 Biblical truths affirming our God will never leave us or forsake us. When you need encouragement, look them up. Write them on cards. Post them in places as a reminder. Memorize them.

1. Deuteronomy 31:6
2. Deuteronomy 31:8
3. Joshua 1:5
4. 1 Kings 8:57
5. 1 Chronicles 28:20
6. Psalms 37:28
7. Psalms 94:14
8. Isaiah 41:17
9. Isaiah 42:16
10. Hebrews 13:5

We need to stretch our faith, trusting God with the future. But it requires us to surrender our will to Him each morning. It's hard, however, to surrender to God's will when we insist on doing things our way.

While two-year-olds may insist on doing things their way, if we are true followers of Christ, we should be doing things His way. If we believe God has a better way of living life, we should have *"confidence in what we hope for and assurance about what we do not see."*

Follow Through

Trust: Is your confidence in God or in your own abilities? Why? Do you have trouble letting go and letting God be in control? What do you think it would look like if you did let go and trust Him completely? Do you pray and ask for God's direction and help before making a major decision? If so, how has it helped you to trust Him more? If you haven't, why not?

Thrive: Have you ever taken a leap of faith? What was it? What happened? Were you afraid or were you trusting God to catch you if you failed?

If you have been afraid to step out of the boat, what would help you to take that first step? What's holding you back?

What small step has God directed you to take recently? Are you resisting because He hasn't revealed His entire plan?

God wants us to trust Him completely. He never reveals His entire plan to any of us, including the great heroes of the Bible, like Abraham, Moses and Joshua.

Treasure: Follow through by copying the 10 scriptures listed in today's devotional. Write them on index cards. Memorize them. Treasure them as affirmation that your Abba Father will never leave you nor forsake you.

WEEK 43

DO YOU HAVE THE COURAGE TO OBEY?

"Have I not commanded you? Be strong and courageous. Do not be afraid; do not be discouraged, for the LORD your God will be with you wherever you go"—Joshua 1:9 (NIV).

"A comfort zone is a beautiful place but nothing ever grows there."

When I saw this quote posted on a friend's Facebook page, I had to share it with others. Curious, I googled the quote to discover the author of the statement. Although many have repeated it, the original source is unknown.

We've all seen similar inspirational quotes encouraging us to get out of our routines and do something we normally wouldn't do. While it's sometimes difficult to push the boundaries of our comfort zones, when we do take that step, we often wonder why it took us so long to cross that barrier.

So, what is a "comfort zone" exactly? It's our tendency to get comfortable with the familiar and our daily routines. It's a place or situation where we feel safe or at ease and without stress.

Examples abound in the Bible of those who left their comfort zone in obedience to God's calling. Abraham struck out for an unknown land, leaving family and friends behind because God had called him to do so. Moses definitely left his comfort zone behind when God called him to lead the Israelites out of Egypt into the Promised Land.

In July 2005, I obeyed God and moved from a small northeastern Oklahoma community, where I'd lived for more than 30 years, to a city approximately 80 miles southwest.

Before relocating, I could count on one hand the number of people I knew in my new place of residence. It was a leap of faith for someone like me who had always played it safe. However, if I hadn't obeyed and left my comfort zone, I would never have experienced the adventures God has led me on.

Joshua 1:9 says, *"Have I not commanded you? Be strong and courageous. Do not be afraid; do not be discouraged, for the Lord your God will be with you wherever you go."*

I recall when two members of my Sunday school class, along with another Christian, traveled to Uganda to teach the people there how to drill their own water wells to save the villagers thousands of dollars. Two years before then, God placed on Tom Varner's heart a desire to build a drill for the Ugandans.

Tom set about with a friend to construct the tool needed to accomplish the goal. With financial assistance from members of our class, Tom and a friend finished the drill bit and shipped it to Uganda. Along with Jerry Smith, a pastor and missionary to Uganda, the three spent eight days teaching the Ugandans how to use the drill to locate water.

When Tom obeyed God, he had no idea where it would lead. But something grew out of that obedience—and it will continue to multiply for generations to follow—all because one person had the courage to step outside his comfort zone.

Follow Through

Trust: What does it mean to you to step outside your comfort zone? To me, it means doing things you don't feel comfortable with doing. After I began writing my weekly column in 2005, I started receiving invitations to speak.

While writing came easy for me, speaking before my peers was outside my comfort zone. I had taught high school for 30 years. I had no problem speaking before a classroom full of teenagers. Put me in front of my peers to speak and my hands would perspire so badly the sweat would literally drip onto the floor. In fact, I tell people God must have a sense of humor because the only "C" I made in college was in speech.

Until my pastor encouraged me to get out of the boat, I turned down speaking engagements before large audiences. Now, I've come to realize that speaking before Christian women's groups is part of God's plan for my life. My ministry is to women—to help them get free from society's expectations, to find freedom in a relationship with Christ and to encourage them to take that next step in their relationship with Him.

Is God calling you to get out of the boat, to leave your comfort zone, to do something bold for His kingdom? Before you refuse His invitation to take that leap of faith, ask yourself why you're afraid? Do you trust Him to take care of you, to provide for you, to protect you and guide you? If you said, "Yes," to those questions, then maybe it's time to take a giant leap of faith. He's there to catch you if you fall.

Thrive: When we follow God's leading, life becomes a new adventure each day. When we obey His calling, we find ourselves taking a leap of faith. Hebrews 11:6 tells us that *"without faith it is impossible to please God, because anyone who comes to Him must believe that He exists and that He rewards those who earnestly seek Him."*

Recall the definition of "thrive" mentioned on page 132. One definition means "to grow or develop vigorously." God wants us to grow in our faith. If we're not trusting Him and taking the next step in our journey of faith, we become stagnant. He wants His children to live a vibrant, vigorous life, dedicated to doing His work in the world.

What can you do to make that happen with His help? What has He placed on your heart? In Monday's devotional, Tom Varner, felt led by the Holy Spirit to design and build a tool to help the poor of Uganda drill their own water wells and save money. He left his comfort zone.

You don't have to go overseas, unless that is what you feel God calling you to do. Pray. Ask the Holy Spirit to reveal the next step God wants you to take. Then, take a giant leap of faith.

Treasure: When you take a giant leap of faith, you'll be surprised at the rewards. What are they?
- A new-found confidence in your relationship with the Lord;
- The treasure of new adventures and new friendships;
- The rewards that come from blessing others, including feeling blessed to be a blessing.

November

Prioritize, Prepare, Persevere

"But seek first the kingdom of God and his righteousness, and all these things will be added to you"— Matthew 6:33(ESV).

In 1989, a youth group at Calvary Reformed Church in Holland, Michigan, read and studied Charles Sheldon's 1896 novel, *In His Steps.*

In the novel, a church's parishioners began to preface every thought and action with a simple but thought-provoking question: "What Would Jesus Do?" As they continued to ask this question and follow through, the church members began to see a difference.

After discussing the novel, the Calvary youth took Sheldon's novel to heart and began to create colorful woven bracelets to wear as a tangible reminder of that powerful question. Others throughout their community began wearing the bracelets. The movement grew from there and by the late 90s, the letters WWJD could be found everywhere: on books, T-shirts and other Christian merchandise. Millions of bracelets were sold.

However, the message of WWJD should never be taken for granted because of overuse. In a *Christianity Today* article by Mike Fleischmann, he says, "I wear a bracelet on my wrist with four letters: WWJD—What Would Jesus Do? This saying has become a guiding principle for many Christians. For me it serves as a moral compass, helping me apply abstract elements of my Christian faith to the practical questions I face each day."

However, to find the right answers, we must read and study scripture. We must understand a less obvious question: What did Jesus do?

Fleischmann looked at the four gospels and discovered seven priorities that guided Jesus. In the CT article titled "7 Priorities that Guided

Jesus' Decisions—they can help us in our daily choices," Fleischmann determined the following about Jesus' decisions:

1. *He sought the Father:* "Jesus demonstrated intimacy with God by seeking him continually in prayer. Forty-five times the gospels tell us that Jesus went alone to pray. Every aspect of his life and ministry was saturated with prayer."

2. *He embraced the outcasts*: "Jesus demonstrated the love of God by accepting the castaways of society. This provoked great disdain from the religious establishment. But Jesus was much less squeamish than most about embracing the sinful and sickly, the unseemly and unimportant."

3. *He restored broken lives*: "By the power of God's Spirit, Jesus provided for people's physical and financial needs (Matt. 14:14-21-21, 17:27). He cast out demons (Luke 4:36), healed broken bodies (Luke 5:17), raised the dead (John 11:1-44), and forgave the sins of the guilty (Matt. 9:6). Jesus proved that God's power is sufficient to meet every need. And the Scriptures promise us that the same power works in and through our lives today (Phil. 2:13)."

4. *He confronted hypocrisy*: "Jesus demonstrated the heart of God by standing against lifeless religion. He openly confronted religious hypocrisy (Matt. 23:13-39), inciting great opposition that ultimately led to his execution. Jesus repeatedly rebuked religious people who buried the true heart of God in their manmade traditions (Matt. 19:3-8, Luke 13:10-17). He cleansed the temple because people were using God's house for their own gain (Luke 19:45-46)."

5. *He taught God's Word*: "Whether addressing curious crowds or the committed core, Jesus took advantage of every teachable moment. He was always helping people discover his Father. He lived and spoke the truth, a perfect expression of God's character (John 1:14). But even though he was the incarnate Word, Jesus often directed people back to the written Word. When a religious expert asked Jesus, 'What must I do to inherit eternal life?' Jesus replied, 'What is written in the Law?'

(Luke 10:25-26). The rich young ruler asked the same question, and Jesus answered him from the Scriptures as well (Matt. 19:16-21)."

6. *He served*: "Service marked Jesus' life from start to finish. He served through sacrifice, putting the needs of others above his own. At the last supper, he put on a towel and washed his disciples' feet (John 13:2-17). His life of service culminated at the cross, where the Son of Man died to pay our spiritual debt."

7. *He equipped leaders*: "Finally, Jesus demonstrated God's character by equipping leaders who continued his mission and changed the world after his departure. He refused to let the ministry pressures of today stop him from identifying and investing in the leaders of tomorrow (Matt. 10:1-4)."

Fleischmann urges his reader to go beyond the fad, asking, "So what would Jesus do?

> "He would seek the Father for the strength and wisdom to embrace, restore, confront, teach, serve and equip the people around Him."

He adds, "These seven priorities should drive us back to the gospels to take a fresh look at how Jesus lived."

In November, we will examine our priorities, prepare to serve and persevere in our walk with Jesus.

WEEK 44

WHAT CAN YOU DO IN 10 SECONDS?

"If you love me, keep my commands"—John 14:15 (NIV).

Dubbed the fastest man on earth, Jamaican sprinter Usain Bolt set the world record for running the 100 meter dash in under 10 seconds with a time of 9.58 in the World Athletics Championship finals in 2009. No man has beaten his record since.

Ten seconds. What can we as Christians do in that brief time that leads to following Jesus in an obedient manner? In his book, *The 10 Second Rule: Following Jesus Made Simple*, author Clare DeGraaf writes, "Most of us would like to think of ourselves as followers of Jesus, but what does that really mean, practically?"

In Luke 9:23, Jesus said, *"Whoever wants to be my disciple must deny themselves and take up their cross daily and follow me."*

Says DeGraaf, "Simply put, it's trusting Jesus enough to say 'no' to what we want, and 'yes' to what he wants. So, then why is it we don't obey him more often than we do?"

During the course of his days, DeGraaf began to notice impressions to do something he was reasonably certain Jesus wanted him to do. "It could be an impression to either do something good for someone or a warning about a sin I was about to commit."

He adds, "Almost simultaneously I would sense another voice whispering to me. 'You don't have time to do that—helping that person could get messy—you can't afford to help them right now.'"

DeGraaf said if he listened to this other voice and thought about it too long "the moment for obedience would pass, often to my relief." DeGraaf finally realized he was actually procrastinating and unintentionally teaching himself the habit of disobedience because he knew every decision to obey would cost him something—time, money, embarrassment, inconvenience or a momentary pleasure denied. By choosing not to obey Jesus, he could avoid all these things.

Then DeGraaf learned about the 10-second rule. "It is," he says, "just doing the next thing you're reasonably certain Jesus wants you to do—and doing it immediately before you change your mind!"

After studying Jesus' teachings, DeGraaf has become more spontaneous to simple obedience when opportunities are sent his way. He says, "The Rule doesn't require you to be absolutely certain an impression is from God before you obey. In fact, I've found that the need for certainty is often the enemy of obedience."

Even if the impression isn't from God, he adds, "You've still done something good for another person."

DeGraff admits he sometimes fails to live by "The Rule." However, it has become easier and has changed the way he responds to others' needs. "It becomes a Christian habit," he adds. "It gives you a place to begin again following Jesus, right now—today, if you've drifted spiritually. It's following Jesus made simple and being led by Jesus, moment by moment, day by day—or even in the next 10 seconds."

If you want to experience the natural consequences of a surrendered life, try the 10-second rule. It might just become a habit—a Godly one.

Follow Through

Prioritize: DeGraaf says that he has become more spontaneous to simple obedience when opportunities are sent his way. He adds, "The Rule doesn't require you to be absolutely certain an impression is from God before you obey. In fact, I've found that the need for certainty is often the enemy of obedience." What does this statement mean to you? Have you ever hesitated to help someone in need because you didn't think you had the time? Did the incident weigh on your heart because you didn't respond at that moment? In your journal, answer these questions and then ask yourself what would have been the outcome if you had obeyed that nudge from the Holy Spirit.

Prepare: What does it mean to prepare? According to dictionary.com, prepare means "to put in proper condition or readiness." We know that athletes must prepare or get in the proper condition to compete. What does that mean for a disciple of Jesus Christ?

If we have chosen to follow Jesus, obeying Him and living for Him, then we must prepare to serve Him by helping others. During the three years of His ministry, Jesus prepared His followers to take over after His death on the cross.

How did He prepare them? The written word wasn't available at the time, so Jesus prepared them by sharing parables and stories to teach them what it meant to follow Him. He healed and served others, including the 12 disciples originally chosen by Him at the beginning of His ministry.

If we are to become a faithful servant of His, we must continually prepare by studying and meditating on God's Holy Word and being in fellowship with other believers.

What have you been doing to prepare? Is there something else you need to be doing to help you become more spontaneous as a faithful follower? If you're uncertain, ask a close friend or your pastor to help you evaluate your preparedness. Make a list in your journal of all the ways you have been preparing. Ask the Holy Spirit to guide you on the next step of your spiritual journey. Listen and jot down in your journal what you perceive as His answer.

Persevere: According to dictionary.com, persevere means "to maintain a purpose in spite of difficulty, obstacles, or discouragement; continue steadfastly."

At the 18th Olympics in Tokyo in 1964, the following was spelled out in lights:

"The most important thing in the Olympic Games is not to win but to take part; just as the most important thing in life is not the triumph but the struggle. The essential thing is … to have fought well."

In James 1:12, we are exhorted to persevere "under trials." James writes:

"Blessed is the one who perseveres under trial because, having stood the test, that person will receive the crown of life that the Lord has promised to those who love him."

It is out of our love for Jesus that we persevere in doing good. It is out of our love that we obey when His Holy Spirit nudges us to reach out to another.

Good works are good because they spring from a faith that is true and lively. Never give up in doing good.

Read the epistles of Paul. As you do, write down any scriptures referring to persevering in your faith. What does it mean to you to persevere in your faith?

WEEK 45

IS IT TIME TO TAKE A GOOD LOOK?

"Let's take a good look at the way we're living. Let's return to the Lord"—*Lamentations 3:40(NIRV).*

Yuck! How long had it been? I didn't know, but I knew it was long overdue.

When I found myself in the mood to do some serious housework, I wasn't looking forward to cleaning my refrigerator. While I had kept up with wiping down the inside surfaces I could see, I wasn't excited about tackling what I knew was probably a mess in the hidden places.

If you've ever cleaned a refrigerator, you know what I'm talking about. Those spills you wiped off of the shelves made their way to the bottom underneath the veggie and fruit drawers. Maybe you planned to get to it later but forgot. Maybe, like me, you're a procrastinator.

How often do we procrastinate when it comes to doing things we'd rather avoid? I know I'm guilty. In the past, I very seldom put things off. It just wasn't in my nature. However, as I have embraced each birthday, I've started to examine what is important. Evidently, I've decided cleaning out the deep recesses of my refrigerator is not a high priority.

Before Jesus got ahold of this woman, I could tell you my priorities didn't line up with His. Instead, I was more concerned about how things appeared on the outside. For example, my house was always clean, so clean you could have eaten off the floors most days. My now-grown sons can tell you I wasn't the easiest mother to live with when it came to keeping our house clean.

Another priority was my exterior. Every hair had to be in place before I would walk out my front door. My make-up had to be perfectly applied and my clothing unwrinkled and spotless, lest I run into someone who might judge me for my appearance. While I still struggle with these things to a certain degree, they're not nearly as important as they once were in my life.

As I removed the items from my refrigerator and freezer to begin a comprehensive scrubbing and disinfecting that day, I began to think how we try to hide our true selves from others. While others thought I had my life all together, inside I was filled with insecurities, doubts and secrets. But God knew.

We may try to camouflage our sins behind a mask or stuff them deep down like the dirt in the bottom of the refrigerator, but no matter how hard we try, we can't conceal them from our Heavenly Father. Nothing is ever *"hidden from [God's] sight"* (Heb. 4:13). He sees each of our failures, thoughts and motivations (1 Sam. 16:7; Luke 12:2-3).

Just as we deep clean our homes and our belongings, we must make the examination of our souls a priority. Socrates once said, "The unexamined life is not worth living for a human being."

As Christians, we should seek God for help in cleansing anything from our lives hindering us from His purpose and plan. Isn't it time to take a good look?

Follow Through

Prioritize: While there's nothing wrong with procrastinating, there are certain things in our life that we should not put off. Return to the beginning of this month (page 142) and reread the "7 Priorities that Guided Jesus' Decisions—They can help us in our daily choices."

As you read, ask yourself, the following questions and respond in your journal:
1. *Do I seek intimacy with God on a regular basis?* What does that mean to you? If you are not spending quality time with Him, how can you make it a priority?
2. *What does it mean to you to embrace the outcasts of society?* I confess I have a problem with this sometimes. If you do too, ask the Holy Spirit to help you improve in this area of service.

3. *How can you help restore broken lives?* What does a broken life look like to you? How can you help others with their physical and financial needs? Think of a time when you were led by the Holy Spirit to help someone in need. How did it make you feel to make a difference in someone's life?

4. *How did Jesus confront hypocrisy?* Look up the scriptures listed in number four on page 144. Write them down in your journal, meditate on them and ask yourself if you've ever been confronted by hypocrisy. How did you respond, if you did? Think about how you would respond if you were confronted by hypocrisy. Does the thought of confrontation bother you? Why or why not?

5. *How can you, as a follower of Jesus, teach God's Word to others?* If you're afraid to share the story of Jesus with others, why? Are you afraid of persecution? Of not knowing enough? How can you address those fears?

6. *Service marked Jesus' life from start to finish. Are you serving others?* Where? How did you get involved in service? Are you content in this service or do you feel the Holy Spirit leading you to serve elsewhere? Where? If you are not currently serving others, ask the Holy Spirit to show you where you can best serve God today? Check out opportunities at your church, in your town or city and even nationally and internationally. Make a list of those people and places that interest you and see what you can do to serve.

7. *Jesus knew He would need to equip leaders to follow in His footsteps after He was gone.* What can you do to equip others to become leaders in the church? Visit with your pastor to find out where you could serve to help equip the leaders of tomorrow.

Prepare: Look back over your answers to the questions above. How can you better prepare to be a more effective Christian witness and servant?

Persevere: If you find you are not comfortable in any area of Christian discipleship or if something is hindering you from taking the next step, ask the Holy Spirit to reveal to you what is holding you back. Is it sin? Confess. Fear? Seek His strength. Whatever it is, don't give up. Persevere.

WEEK 46

DO YOU KNOW WHAT
TOMORROW WILL BRING?

"How do you know what is going to happen tomorrow? For the length of your lives is as uncertain as the morning fog—now you see it; soon it is gone"— James 4:14 (TLB).

"I have all the time in the world." After reading this quote from a 25-year-old, who had just won a six-figure payout in a tournament competition, I wanted to tell him, "No, you don't."

His comment was in response to a reporter's question about the young man's plans for the prize money he had won. He planned to save it, for now, according to the newspaper article, but was considering a vacation with a college friend.

While some of us may live 100-plus years, others are taken away much too soon. My heart was sick for the loss of an elderly neighbor and friend. In his late 80s, Dave was killed in a car accident in late May 2017. His wife, Josie, had to undergo surgery for a broken leg and multiple complications as a result of an infection. Her prognosis is good, but her recovery will be a long one.

My last glimpse of them had been that morning when they drove by my house. They waved and Dave honked as I was standing in my front yard visiting with other neighbors. I didn't know it would be the last time I would ever see him—at least on earth.

This couple has experienced their own share of loss. Before they met and married, each had lost spouses at an early age. Dave had also lost a daughter to cancer. He once said to me, "You're not supposed to outlive your children."

I've known other parents who've outlived their children, including a family who lost two sons. It's something I pray I never have to face. But none of us knows what tomorrow will bring. Only God does.

The day of our death will not be a matter of chance. The Bible tells us our days are numbered and scripture makes it clear our lives are in God's hands. In Job 14:5, we read, *"Our time on earth is brief; the number of our days is already decided by you."*

We don't have all the answers to the complex questions about death, but we know someday, we will die. I think the question we need to ask is, "Are you prepared for that day?"

Have you given your life to Christ, trusting Him and asking Him to forgive you for your sins? Have you made a personal commitment to follow Him? I shudder to think what those who don't understand the importance of this commitment will face when they die.

What about your loved ones? Have you shared the message of our precious Savior's sacrifice on the cross? Do they know Jesus came to give us life—right now and in the world to come? Do they have the comfort of knowing where they will spend eternity?

When we know Christ, we can say, just as the psalmist did, *"My times are in your hands" (Psalm 31:15). Jesus came to give us eternal life.*

Have you accepted His invitation?

Follow Through

Prioritize: None of us knows what tomorrow will bring. In light of eternity, what are you doing to make sure others have heard the Good News about Jesus? If not, ask yourself, "Why?"

Prepare: Our times are in God's hands. We don't know when our life or the lives of our loved ones will end. It's not a matter of when, because we know we will all die at some time. It's a matter of being prepared for eternity, an eternity either with or without Jesus. How are you preparing for eternity? Have you given your life to Christ, trusting Him and asking Him to forgive you of your sins? Have you made a personal commitment to follow Him?

Persevere: One of my family members has rejected my attempts to share my faith in Jesus Christ. At one time, it caused a tension in our relationship until God led me to pack up my belongings, sell my house and return to the town where I once lived and this family member resides. Following the Holy Spirit's leading, I've begun to reach out again.

Almost 11 years have passed since that initial rejection. I've grown spiritually. I'm more prepared to share my testimony. I have persevered in my desire to see this family member come to Christ. While it hasn't happened yet, I will not give up.

Are you or have you faced a similar situation? What are you doing or what did you do to share the message of our precious Savior's sacrifice on the cross and what it means for that person's eternal life? Never give up. We never know what tomorrow will bring.

WEEK 47

BUT GOD, I WANT IT NOW!

"And patience develops strength of character in us and helps us trust God more each time we use it until finally our hope and faith are strong and steady"—Romans 5:4(TLB).

Were we more patient before our society became so complicated? What do I mean? For example, before the microwave became a household staple and fast food restaurants graced every corner, weren't we more content to wait when our meals took an hour or more to prepare?

While a watched pot never boils, we lose interest if a frozen meal doesn't open itself and get nuked in less than five minutes. Can't we agree that home-cooked meals are definitely worth the wait?

Before computers, cell phones and social media became everyday fare, weren't we more content to get our news in the daily newspaper and on the five o'clock news? We didn't have the capability to check a Facebook or Twitter feed to keep up with the running commentary of breaking news.

Oh, and what about the download speed of our tech gadgets? If the website doesn't open fast enough or the text message doesn't arrive in warp-speed time, we stomp our feet and curse the aliens in control of cyberspace.

Recently, I was having problems with my cell phone. I wasn't receiving texts from a friend. I would anxiously await a reply and when none would come, I would grow impatient. However, I soon discovered the new community to which I had moved didn't have the best coverage for my cell carrier. I also discovered my phone needed a reboot when I stopped by a cell phone store concerning another problem. After the technician demonstrated the solution, nine text messages arrived. All were from the same friend and covered a two-day span.

Another friend, who broke her ankle recently, is learning a valuable lesson in patience. Each time she has pushed herself during the healing process, she has had a setback. We've discussed patience and the importance of God's timing during this process.

Look up the definition of patience and you'll find the following: "the capacity to accept or tolerate delay, trouble, or suffering without getting angry or upset."

What is interesting is that the word has the same root as the word "patient, "which means suffering. Impatient people often think they are suffering when they can't have what they want, now.

Christian theologian and philosopher Augustine once said, "Patience is the companion of wisdom."

In Proverbs 9:10 (TLB), King Solomon writes, *"For the reverence and fear of God are basic to all wisdom. Knowing God results in every other kind of understanding."*

As we grow in God's wisdom, patience follows. At least it has for me. That doesn't mean I'm always patient, but as I tell a friend, "I'm a whole lot better than I used to be."

Businessman and author Arnold Glasow once wrote, "The key to everything is patience. You get the chicken by hatching the egg, not by smashing it."

Learning patience is an ongoing process, requiring us to trust God more each day.

Follow Through

Prioritize: When our priorities are out-of-sync with God's, we rush through life trying to accomplish our goals in our timing. We want it now! Do you think technology has made our society more impatient? Why or why not? Look at your own life prior to some of today's technological advances. Do you think life was less hurried? Were you more patient? Reflect on these questions in your journal.

Prepare: Copy Romans 5:4 in your journal. Meditate on this scripture's relevance to your life. Ask yourself if you are as patient as you want to be. Has your patience developed through the years? If it has, to what do you attribute the increase in your patience. If not, ask yourself, "Why?" Ask God to help you develop more patience.

Persevere: Learning patience is an ongoing process. About the time I think I've arrived, I take a step backwards. Do you experience the same? Remind yourself to persevere. Pray for God's Holy Spirit to help you persevere in the midst of your impatience. In your journal, reflect on the times you've remained patient in the face of opposition or adversity. How might you have acted earlier in your walk with the Lord? Do you give God the credit for helping you to become a more patient person? Why or why not?

WEEK 48

CAN YOU FIND YOUR IDENTITY
IN FOUR WORDS?

"But to all who believed him and accepted him, he gave the right to become children of God"—John 1:12(NLT).

If someone asked you to identify yourself in four words, could you do it? Recently, on a social media site, participants answered that question. I did, too. My response was, "A child of God."

Before I turned to God during a life-changing event over 16 years ago, I couldn't make that statement. Before I found my identity in Christ, I would have said I was a daughter, a wife, a mother, a high school teacher and a professional photographer. My identity was wrapped up in my earthly relationships and my professions. While those aren't negative identities, they defined who I thought I was.

In my late 40s, I began asking, "Who am I?" I was lost. When God revealed my true identity in Him, I discovered how much God loves me and wanted a relationship with me. The shackles fell off. I was free to be the person He created me to be.

When we find our identity in Christ, He begins to work in our hearts. How?

First, you're no longer a slave to other's opinions. Before my identity change, I was a people pleaser, which isn't emotionally, mentally or spiritually healthy.

Second, embracing your new identity in Christ leads to a change of priorities. Afraid God will expect them to change, some people refuse to accept His offer of grace. He does. However, when He performs a heart transplant on you, you want to change. It's not overnight, but a gradual awakening of His love for us that leads to a makeover in His image.

2 Corinthians 5:17 says, *"Therefore, if anyone is in Christ, the new creation has come: The old has gone, the new is here!"*

A third change involves the comfort we receive when we take on our new identity. Psalm 34:18 says, *"The Lord is close to the brokenhearted and saves those who are crushed in spirit."*

As you grow into your new identity, you experience more peace. As He has revealed Himself to me through scripture, I've learned to trust Him, no matter the situation. While life isn't necessarily easier, I'm able to face the challenges, knowing God will use it for His glory.

As a child of God, I've also discovered a renewed strength, especially in situations I never expected to face. He is *"the strength of my heart and my portion forever* (Psalm 73:26).

In March 2016, I found myself huddled in a bedroom closet with my dog clutched to my chest. The tornado siren was blaring. In the past, I would have been paralyzed with fear. I wasn't. Even as the tornado hit my house, I continued to pray. When the winds died down and all was calm, I was enveloped in a peace only a child of God can understand.

Although it took me over 40 years to find that peace, I can say, without reservation, "I am a child of God."

Follow Through

Prioritize: Have you ever examined your priorities in life? As you think about this question, list your priorities in your journal. Do you derive your identity from your job? Is your job a priority over your family? Is your family a priority over time spent with your Abba Father? Why or why not? Examine your life in light of eternity. If you had 24 hours to live, what would you do differently during that time?

Prepare: Are you prepared for the "tornadoes" of life—those times when you find yourself taking cover and praying for an end to the trials? Preparation for the trials means seeking God in advance by spending quality time meditating on scripture and listening for that still, small voice that brings a peace like no other. Growing spiritually through fellowship with other Christians and spending time in prayer also strengthens you for this journey called life.

Ask yourself the following questions:
1. Do I spend more time on social media or on my cell phone than with God?
2. Has my time with God become stale?
3. Am I going through the motions? Do I need something to revitalize my time with Him?
4. Am I spending time with God out of guilt?
5. Do I find myself looking at my watch, hurrying to finish so I can move on to my to-do-list?

Persevere: Even mature Christians hit road bumps and lose their zeal. The Christian life is not always a smooth one. However, we can't grow without the storms in our lives. We grow in the valleys, not on the mountaintops.

Spending time in God's Word isn't about gaining more knowledge. In this information age, we're bombarded with facts as well as "fake" news. Our faith is about a living, breathing relationship with our Heavenly Father.

Psalm 25:4 says, *"Show me your ways, Lord, teach me your paths."*

Just as our earthly father and mother teach us the ways of this world, a relationship with the Lord teaches us the ways of His Kingdom. It's an ongoing process. We must intentionally schedule time with Him just as we schedule other appointments in our life. Just as it does in any relationship, it takes effort to find time and energy to connect with God on a regular basis.

If your time with Him becomes stale, change things up. Find a new devotional guide. Purchase a different version of the Bible. Try prayer journaling or some other method to connect on a deeper level with God.

Do you identify yourself as a "child of God?" Is your hope in Him? If not, what is holding you back? Seek His face until you find your identity in Him, and Him alone.

December

Search, Serve, Shine

"You will seek me and find me when you seek me with all your heart"— Jeremiah 29:13(NIV).

S earch, as a verb, according to dictionary.com, means "to go or look through (a place, area, etc.) carefully in order to find something missing or lost."

As a noun, search is "an act of searching for someone or something."

Have you ever been lost or lost someone or something? I have. And not just in the physical sense. What do I mean? If you've read this far, you know that before discovering I could have a living, intimate relationship with my Savior and Lord, I was hopelessly lost in this secular world.

I never knew what it meant to be loved unconditionally. I lived to please others. I feared failure and rejection if I didn't say or do the right thing. I never felt "good" enough. I never felt as if I fit in unless I compromised the person God intended for me to be. Although I had moments of happiness, I never experienced true joy until I surrendered my life to Christ.

What about you? Have you surrendered your life to the One who loves you without reservation, who died on the cross for your sins, who wants you to live in eternity with Him?

Reread the previous sentence. Isn't the thought of His bloody sacrifice enough to bring you to your knees?

If you're searching for the perfect life, you won't find it anywhere on this planet. However, through a personal relationship with Jesus, you can find perfect peace.

Jesus begins working in our hearts before we ever start seeking Him. Luke 19:10 says, *"For the Son of Man came to seek and to save the lost."*

Once you've accepted Him into your heart and life, a change occurs. It's not an overnight event, but a gradual awakening of feeling loved and being accepted for the person you are without the mask of insecurity.

Although I've always loved helping others, as I drew closer to Jesus through reading scripture, Bible studies, prayer and fellowship with other believers, I wanted to serve in other ways. I began to attend church regularly, participated in mission trips inside and outside the country, and volunteered through different church activities. One that is close to my heart is working in our church's food pantry.

Through serving others, we become the hands and feet of Jesus. His light shines through us as we seek ways to glorify Him through our words and actions.

What about you? Are you ready during this time when we celebrate His birth to search, serve and shine? However, don't let it end there. Seek His guidance each morning and ask, "Lord, where can I serve You today?

WEEK 49

WHEN YOU ARE BLESSED

"The generous will themselves be blessed, for they share their food with the poor" –Proverbs 22:9 (NIV).

Positive news from the media always attracts my attention in this negative, broken world. It's especially uplifting to hear of the good deeds of others, even when that individual is in the midst of disappointment or pain.

I recall a news report several years ago about the story of a young woman in Colorado Springs whose wedding ceremony was called off two days before the planned event. Instead of focusing on herself, the young woman decided to use the occasion to bless others.

The bride-to-be's parents had planned a lavish Saturday night feast after the ceremony. Instead of letting the food go to waste, the young woman told her parents she wanted to feed the less fortunate, many of whom are homeless. With the help of the Salvation Army, the family used this opportunity to reach out to others and surprise them with an early Thanksgiving dinner.

A Salvation Army representative said the hot meal on a very cold night also warmed many hearts. "In all my years, I have never seen anything like this," he said.

Although the young woman was not interviewed on camera, the father had this to say about his daughter. "She is a super giving young lady. I have been blessed with two wonderful daughters and was not surprised when she chose to do this."

We make choices each day, some good and some not so good. However, every decision we make has consequences. One choice that will radically change your life and those around you is the one that recognizes the world does not revolve around you. We are here for a purpose and the greatest joy in life comes when we are set free to meet the needs of others.

Talking with a new friend about his trips to the Ukraine in the former USSR, Brian described his travels and the people he had met. He said, "After visiting the Ukraine, I realized I was more materialistic than I thought."

Commenting on the smiles he saw on the faces of the Ukrainians, Brian said, "I wondered how they could be so happy when they had so little."

Having traveled to Mexico on my first mission trip in 2008, I could relate to Brian's statement. Even in the midst of poverty, I saw contentment through the smiles of the poorest.

I also saw those same radiant smiles on the faces of those who lived in the most poverty-stricken areas of Israel in 2010. Even in their lack, they appeared richer than many in our country where our wants have become necessities.

As we begin this holiday season, let's remember to give thanks by sharing with others who are less fortunate and begin Advent celebrating the birth of Jesus Christ and not focusing on material things.

The rush to grab our hard-earned dollars starts earlier each year. While there is nothing wrong with buying presents and getting a bargain, don't forget others who have so much less than you.

Follow Through

Search: If you're tired of the commercialism surrounding this holiday, find a place to serve through your church, an organization or in your community.

Serve: After serving or helping someone less fortunate, journal your thoughts. Keep serving in that area or others even after the holidays end. What has serving taught you?

Shine: Think about the reactions and the facial expressions of those you served. How did you feel about blessing them?

WEEK 50

HAVE A HUNDRED-DOLLAR HOLIDAY

"Then he said to them, "Watch out! Be on your guard against all kinds of greed; a man's life does not consist in the abundance of his possessions"—Luke 12:15 (NIV).

If you ask any American child what he likes about Christmas, you would probably hear the same answer. In their excitement, most would probably shout the word "presents" or "toys."

Ask any harried parent what he likes about Christmas and I believe you would get a different answer. You would get even another viewpoint if you asked retailers.

The Christmas season is upon us. Although the advertising blitz has been going on for a few months—or at least it feels that way—I find it hard to get excited. I don't think I am alone.

If you asked me to describe the perfect holiday season, I would include the following: the company of loved ones, good food, fun and relaxation, and maybe a few inches of snow. Although my wish list seems simple, for many, this ideal could not be farther from reality.

Too often, the holidays seem to exhaust us because we feel trapped by the shopping, spending, and frenzied preparations when we should feel uplifted. A recent national survey revealed that 70 percent of Americans long for less emphasis on gift giving and spending.

In his 1998 book titled *Hundred Dollar Holiday: The Case for a More Joyful Christmas*, Bill McKibben offers a simple proposal in the midst of the holiday madness. He suggests spending only $100 (total) on Christmas, and instead of shopping, we should spend time with the people we love.

Critics of McKibben have called him the Grinch that stole Christmas.

Responding to the criticism, McKibben said, "I've been called my share of names, but the only one that ever really stung was 'Grinch.'"

It was with apprehension that McKibben picked up his daughter's well-worn copy of the Dr. Seuss classic and reread the popular tale. After rereading the story, McKibben found new understanding.

In Seuss's book, the Grinch hears the sound of singing on Christmas morning and realizes he has not stopped Christmas at all

> *"And the Grinch, with his grinch-feet ice-cold in the snow,*
> *Stood puzzling and puzzling: "How could it be so?*
> *It came without ribbons! It came without tags!*
>
> *"It came without packages, boxes or bags!*
> *And he puzzled three hours, `till his puzzler was sore.*
> *Then the Grinch thought of something he hadn't before!*
> *'Maybe Christmas,' he thought, 'doesn't come from a store.*
> *Maybe Christmas...perhaps...means a little bit more!'"*

Wouldn't it be nice if more people realized that Christmas doesn't come from a store and is maybe...perhaps...a little bit more?

In a society, where material goods are bountiful but quality time is not, I think McKibben has a great idea. If we start putting the "peace of mind" back into Christmas with a spending limit, we will find, just like the Grinch, that the true meaning of Christmas was right under our noses the whole time.

As you make your holiday shopping list, remember the old cliché: "Jesus is the reason for the season."

Follow Through

Search: Has the Christmas season become synonymous with overspending for you? Do you dread the commercialism? What can you do, as an individual and as a family, to create your ideal holiday that is filled with peace, instead of the hurried rush to get ready?

Serve: Seek ways to serve with your family this Christmas season. Could you volunteer to serve a meal at a homeless shelter? Maybe you could make cookies and share them with local nursing home residents. Sit down as a family and create a list of ideas to make this Christmas season more meaningful?

Shine: At the beginning of the season, set a limit on what you will spend. Have you ever heard of giving your children just three gifts? Since I have six grandchildren and I am on a fixed income, I now give each child the following: one gift of their choice, a book and one piece of clothing. Guess what? They love it! And, I'm not left in holiday credit card debt.

What can you do to give more meaningful gifts?

WEEK 51

DON'T FORGET TO K.I.S.S.

"This will be a sign to you: You will find a baby wrapped in cloths and lying in a manger--Luke 2:12 (NIV).

Do you know how to K.I.S.S.? I do. However, it's taken me years to learn. To keep it simple, that is. Several years ago, a small newspaper item caught my attention because the headline was titled "Local Church Reminds People to KISS."

K.I.S.S. is an acronym for Keep it Simple, Stupid. The church, however, was offering a one-day workshop to encourage people to keep it simple and sacred during the holiday season.

To remind everyone about the true meaning of the season, the church was providing ways to have a simple and sacred Christmas celebration. Kids were invited to bring an adult and make a Snowman Advent calendar. Adults also had the opportunity to buy an alternative Christmas gift from Heifer International.

I can remember trick-or-treating for UNICEF, an organization benefitting children worldwide. The organization still exists but you don't hear as much about it today.

What you do hear, even before the stores have cleared their Halloween merchandise, is the sound of Christmas bells. Somewhere between the scary costumes and the artificially decorated trees, we have forgotten to give thanks.

In our rush to start celebrating a season that has become too commercialized, we are caught up in the flurry of secular activities. What would Jesus think?

In the past decade, I decided to be more like Mary who sat at Jesus' feet, instead of Martha, stressed with her preparations for His visit. I don't want to criticize Martha because I used to be like her. Having the

~169~

perfectly decorated tree and house, rushing to one holiday activity after another and stressing about the perfect gift left me so frazzled I couldn't enjoy the season.

I recall a phone conversation with a friend who reminded me of this annual scenario. She said, "This year I'm not going to run around trying to make everything perfect for my family, even if they demand it. I'm going to enjoy this time with family and friends, remember the real reason for Christmas and keep it more holy."

What if each one of us made that choice? Wouldn't it be wonderful? I love this time of the year—the smell of a freshly cut tree, the sound of the Salvation Army bells, the taste of fudge and banana bread, the sight of twinkling lights—but I dislike the advertising blitz that leaves me feeling like I've been run over by a runaway sleigh full of intoxicated elves.

I'm not a Christmas Grinch. I love seeing the smiling eyes when a gift I have chosen brings joy to a loved one or friend. It's the greatest present I receive at this time of year.

Start a new tradition this year. Set a limit on your spending and stay away from more credit card debt. Avoid the malls and enjoy just being with your family and friends. Better yet, make your own gifts.

Remember God's Son and our Savior. He's the sacred reason for this season.

Follow Through

Search: Search for ways to make your Christmas season more sacred. If your church doesn't offer any workshops or opportunities to do so, start or suggest ways to do so. For example, have a workshop like the one mentioned in this devotional where children can make their own Advent calendar. Look on Pinterest or other DIY sites to come up with ideas. Don't stop there. What else can you do to make this season more about Jesus and less about shopping? Brainstorm with your church family and friends for ideas.

Serve: Look for ways to serve others as a church family. What about

Christmas caroling at local nursing homes? If your community has a Christmas parade, maybe you could enter a float or set up a roadside stand at the end of the parade route and give away free cups of hot chocolate. Think of other ways to serve your community as a church family.

Shine: As you serve with your church and family members, notice the reactions of others—both those who are serving and those you are serving. Are you experiencing the blessing of being a blessing? Do you think the others involved are also experiencing that same blessing?

WEEK 52

WHAT ARE YOU GIVING TO JESUS?

"For God so loved the world that he gave His one and only Son..."—John 3:16 (NIV).

Sometimes Christmas does not fit our expectations of what the perfect holiday should be. We decorate our homes, inside and out. We shop. We wrap gifts. We plan parties or dinners. We attend other holiday events.

The days leading up to Christmas pass by faster than the ding of cash registers filling up with cash and credit card receipts. After the wrapping paper is discarded, we can be left with an emptiness that no store-bought gift can fill.

In his book, *Christmas spirit: Memories of Family, Friends and Faith*, pastor Joel Osteen writes, "When Christmas doesn't fit your expectations of what the perfect holiday should be, think about how Joseph and Mary probably didn't think the manger was the perfect place for their child to be born. But look at what a perfect Christmas it turned out to be."

A recent devotional I read was a reminder to seek the real meaning of Christmas. The writer shared a time before Christmas when her husband accidentally broke one of her favorite porcelain teacups while washing dishes. The delicate cup had shattered into so many pieces that glue could not restore it to its original purpose. The tea would have leaked out. Regretfully, she tossed the cup into the trash.

However, on Christmas morning, an unexpected gift of love from her nine-year-old son brought tears to her eyes. Although she had forgotten about the broken teacup, her son had retrieved the pieces from the trash and painstakingly glued them back together.

Because the young boy knew how much his mother loved the cup, he had taken time to put it back together. Chipped and scarred with dried glue oozing through some of the cracks, the restored teacup was beautiful in the mother's eyes. Although it would no longer hold tea, it was a reminder to her of the true meaning of Christmas.

The literal meaning of Christmas is "Christ's Mass," referring to a celebration of Christ. However, our current culture doesn't reflect the wonder and awe of that first Christmas over 2,000 years ago. While we search for a joyful Christmas that truly celebrates Christ, so often the season leaves us with very little joy and an elusive emptiness we can't seem to define.

I recall having lunch with two friends where our discussion centered on this season. We talked about the needy in our community, especially the children who would not have much at Christmas if it were not for the benevolence of others.

If you want to know the secret to a Christmas holiday filled with love, peace and joy, then look to the manger. The very heart of Christmas came wrapped in swaddling clothes. He was a gift from our Heavenly Father. God loved us so much He sent His only Son that we might be restored to wholeness.

It is Jesus' birthday we celebrate on December 25, not ours. What gift can you give the Christ child? Start by examining your heart, asking yourself what you can do to help others have a more blessed life.

Giving sacrificially is what Jesus demonstrated. Let us be reminded of that and model His servant's heart.

Follow Through

Search: Search for ways to be a blessing to others without spending much or any money. Listen to the hearts of others and you'll discover what they truly treasure. Think about the little boy who tried to repair his mother's broken teacup. It wasn't the physical gift but the gift that came from the heart that meant so much to this mother.

Serve: What gifts can you give your family and friends this Christmas without spending much or any money? Make a list. Below is a partial one to get you started. (Credit goes to tinygreenmom.com)

Gifts and ideas that don't cost anything or cost very little:

• Write a letter telling each family member what they mean to you. Put it on nice paper and frame it in an inexpensive second hand store frame with a photo of the recipient.

• Make CD's of your favorite music selections personalized for the recipient. Don't use pirated music.

• Offer a coupon to be a work-out partner for a friend or relative and keep each other accountable for your exercise goals. What is better than planned time with people who are important to you and you can get healthier in the process?

• Give the family heirlooms away before you die. Instead of keeping Grandmother's crystal in the cupboard give this special family gift to others to use and enjoy.

• Give a coupon to wash windows this spring…or some other dreaded job.

• Give your kids a coupon for one week of no bed making or other hated chore.

• Make Christmas ornaments using school or family pictures of loved ones and decorate them with ribbon or felt.

• Have an ugly ornament exchange. Everyone brings an ugly ornament to hang on the tree and then a vote is held for the most notorious.

• Give the gift of time to attend events by giving coupons for activities for an elderly family member or young child.

• For the family member that has everything, make a donation in their name to a special charity or a charity of their choice.

• For the writers in your family create a journal with notebooks, paper and a front cover decorated with a photo.

• Start a scrapbook of family or friend photos and give it to the recipient to continue to add to through the year.

• Offer to babysit for the young couple on your list.

• Give an inexpensive recipe box filled with family recipes. Or do this one better and give a recipe and all the fixings to make a special meal or dessert.

Shine: Bake a birthday cake for Jesus and serve it with your Christmas meal. Sing Happy Birthday to Jesus and ask Him to shine through you each day of the year.

WORKS CITED

Ashcraft, Mike, and Rachel Olsen. *My One Word: Change Your Life with Just One Word*. Zondervan, 2013.

Brown, Brene. *Daring Greatly: How the Courage to Be Vulnerable Transforms the Way We Live, Love, Parent, and Lead*. Penguin Books Ltd, 2016.

Bruner, Kay E. *As Soon as I Fell: a Memoir*. Createspace Publishing Platform, 2014.

Cloud, Steven B. "A Year of Time." Vol. 14, #2, Pulpit Helps, June 2004, www.pulpithelps.com.

Ehman, Karen. *Keep It Shut: What to Say, How to Say It, and When to Say Nothing at All*. Zondervan, 2015.

Fleischmann, Mike. "7 Priorities That Guided Jesus' Decisions—They Can Help Us in Our Daily Choices." *Christianity Today*, May 2013.

Geisel, Theodor Seuss. *How the Grinch Stole Christmas*. Random House, 1957.

Graaf, Clare De. *The 10-Second Rule: Following Jesus Made Simple*. Howard Books, 2013.

McBratney, Sam, et al. *Guess How Much I Love You*. Magi Publications, 2003.

McKibben, Bill. *Hundred Dollar Holiday: the Case for a More Joyful Christmas*. Simon & Schuster, 2013.

Michel, Jen Pollock. "What We Get Wrong About the Desires of Our Heart." *Relevant* magazine.

Omartian, Stormie. *Power of Praying for Your Adult Children Book of Prayers*. Harvest House Publishers, 2014.

Piper, Watty. *Little Engine That Could*. Platt & Munk , 1905.

WORKS CITED

Shook, Kerry, and Chris Shook. *One Month to Live: Thirty Days to a No-Regrets Life*. WaterBrook Press, 2012.

Strobel, Lee. *The Case for Easter: a Journalist Investigates the Evidence for the Resurrection*. Zondervan, 2004.

Upchurch, John. "7 Daily Steps to Trust in the Lord with All Your Heart." *Bible Study Tools*, 15 Mar. 2015, www.biblestudytools.com/.

Warren, Rick. *The Purpose Driven Life: What on Earth Am I Here for?* Zondervan, 2002.

ABOUT THE AUTHOR

CAROL ROUND, self-syndicated columnist, Christian author and inspirational speaker, began her journey with the Lord in October 2001 when she admitted her need for His guidance. Since then, she has sought a deeper relationship with Him through reading scripture, Bible study and the personal discipline of keeping a daily prayer journal.

After being encouraged by other Christian women, she penned a book to encourage others to try prayer journaling. Released in 2012, *Journaling with Jesus: How to Draw Closer to God* and the companion workbook, *The 40-Day Challenge*, can be purchased through the author or on Amazon.com.

Carol has also authored three collections of her weekly faith-based column. *A Matter of Faith*, and *Faith Matters*, was released by Buoy Up Press. A third collection, *Sola Fide: by FAITH alone*, debuted in 2012. She has been writing her weekly faith-based column since 2005. It now runs in 14 Oklahoma newspapers, several national publications and at http://www.assistnews.net/.

"The most amazing part of this journey for me," she says, "happened when ASSIST News, a California publication, started carrying my weekly column five years ago. Because of this worldwide exposure, my column has been picked up by different foreign newspapers and magazines. I'm truly humbled by the feedback I receive from my readers, including those from around the world—India, Uganda, Belfast, Australia, Great Britain, France, Kenya, New Zealand, Ireland and many more. It is truly God at work in my life!"

Carol's writing has led to a speaking ministry. "When I speak to women, I love telling them, 'God has a sense of humor.' While I could stand in front of a classroom full of teenagers when I taught school, getting up in front of my peers terrified me. In fact, the only 'C' I made in college was in speech.

"I've learned God doesn't call the equipped but equips the called. I say all of this in humility because this was not my plan for life after a public education career. But I love using my gifts for His glory."

After 30 years in public education, Carol retired in 2005, knowing God had other plans for her life. Did you know you won't find the word, "retirement," in the Bible? "I call it redirection and love to remind others who are close to retirement or retired to seek God's redirection for their lives."

The mother of two grown sons, Carol is also "Nana" to six adorable and talented grandchildren and the obedient owner of a spoiled rotten dog named Harley, a Chihuahua/Daschund mix, better known as a Chiweenie.

When Carol isn't writing or speaking, she loves spending time with her grandchildren, shooting photos, volunteering at her church, getting her hands dirty in her flowerbeds and hiking.

To learn more about Carol, you can visit her blog/website at **http://carolaround.com**. You can also find her on the following social media sites:

Personal Facebook page at https://www.facebook.com/carolaround

Author Facebook page at
https://www.facebook.com/authorCarolRound/

Facebook <u>book</u> pages include the following:

https://www.facebook.com/JournalingwithJesus

https://www.facebook.com/pages/A-Matter-of-Faith/132121790200971

https://www.facebook.com/pages/Nanas-3-Jars/580643468748234

Twitter: https://twitter.com/carolaround

I always love hearing from my readers. Please feel free to email me at **carol@carolaround.com** or contact me through social media or my website.

And remember, we authors appreciate your feedback through reviews on Amazon. If this book has made a difference in your relationship with Jesus, would you please leave a review and recommend it to your friends?

Devotional Books
by Carol Round

A Matter of Faith
ISBN-13: 978-1543294279 124 pages $9.95
Available from Amazon.com and other online retailers

In this collection of her faith-based columns, Carol Round uses everyday experiences to inspire her readers to seek a deeper relationship with the Lord. Her weekly faith-based column is currently available in 12 Oklahoma newspapers and several on-line publications, including http://www.assistnews.net/. Her columns are also frequently picked up by foreign publications. Readers can also read her columns at **www.carolaround.com**.

Faith Matters
ISBN-10: 0937660833 124 pages $9.95
Available from Amazon.com and other online retailers

Carol Round's weekly faith-based column, "A Matter of Faith," has inspired over 200,000 readers since it first debuted in November 2005. About her second collection, Amazon reviewer Donald Mitchell says, "Ms. Round has the nice ability to meld Biblical inspiration with everyday humility to see new wonders of living through our Lord, Jesus Christ."

by FAITH alone
ISBN-13:978-1479252275 216 pages $12.95
Available from Amazon.com and other online retailers

Since the release of her first collection of columns in 2007, and the global exposure to her weekly faith-based column, "A Matter of Faith," readers continue to express their gratitude for Ms. Round's inspirational work. In this, her third collection of columns, she once again captures hearts and encourages others to grow spiritually through a personal relationship with Jesus.

Books for Spiritual Growth
by Carol Round

Journaling with Jesus: How to Draw Closer to God
ISBN-10: 1449736610   84 pages $9.95
Available from Amazon.com and other online retailers

"Journaling with Jesus" is a creative call to an authentic, intimate relationship
with Christ through the art of prayer-journaling. The author openly shares her
own intimate journaling journey, initially borne of pain, and now bathed in
promises—the hope of healing in Jesus. Allow "Journaling with Jesus" to take
you deep into the heart of God, by showing you practically and inspirationally
how to bare the depths of your own heart on the blank page. As you fill your
journal with words of honesty, God will fill your heart with the wonder of His
love.

The 40 Day Challenge: A companion workbook to Journaling with Jesus: How to Draw Closer to God
ISBN-10: 0615691714   60 pages $12.95
Available from Amazon.com and other online retailers

Are you as close to God as you would like to be? The 40-Day Challenge is a
companion workbook to "Journaling with Jesus: How to Draw Closer to God,"
which challenges readers to try prayer journaling for 40 days.

Children's Books
by Carol Round

Nana's 3 Jars: Giving Generously
ISBN-13: 978-0692280195   21 pages $12.95
Available from Amazon.com and other online retailers

Charlie and Emma are excited. A day spent in the country with their Nana
turns into an opportunity to learn about the joy of giving when they make
chocolate chip cookies to hand out to veterans at a local center. Join Charlie
and Emma as they learn about Nana's 3 Jars and why the 'giving' jar is extra
special. "Nana's 3 Jars: Giving Generously" is an interactive book for adults to
read with and then make cookies with children using the recipe in the back of
the book.

Nana's 3 Jars: Saving Pennies
ISBN-13: 978-1507770788   20 pages $12.95
Available from Amazon.com and other online retailers

Charlie and Emma are excited about spending a fall day with their Nana in the
country where they learn how to save pennies by buying apples from a
Farmer's Market to make their own applesauce. "Nana's 3 Jars: Saving
Pennies" is another interactive book for adults to read with and then make
applesauce with children using the recipe in the back of the book.

Nana's 3 Jars: Spending Wisely
ISBN-13: 978-0692532423   23 pages $12.95
Available from Amazon.com and other online retailers

Charlie has a dilemma. Christmas is approaching and he wants to give his
teacher a special gift. He's been saving his money to purchase a present for
Miss James but until he and Emma make a trip to visit Nana, he isn't quite
sure what he will do. Join Charlie and Emma as they learn more about the
third jar — spending wisely — and why it's just as important as the giving and
saving jars. "Nana's 3 Jars: Spending Wisely" is an interactive book for adults
to read and then make hot chocolate mix with children using the recipe in the
back of the book. It is the third and final book in the "Nana's 3 Jars" series.

ONE FINAL WORD FROM THE AUTHOR

Like all authors, I depend on my readers to get the word out about my books. I don't write for the money. I write because of my love of the Lord and because He has called me to minister to women through my writing and speaking.

How can you help?

1. Buy extra copies of this book for your female friends and relatives. Contact me for discounts or order directly from Amazon.

2. Share your copy with others.

3. Leave a review at amazon.com. Here is a link to my author's page at Amazon: **https://www.amazon.com/Carol-Round/e/B0083ZEAWI.** You can also google "Carol Round books at Amazon," which should take you directly to the link where you can find a list of all my books and the anthologies to which I have contributed.

4. If this book has impacted your life, please let me know at **carol@carolaround.com.** Your feedback encourages me to continue doing what I do.

5. If you would like to receive my weekly column/devotional which appears in 14 Oklahoma newspapers, several national publications and in ASSIST News, an international publication, please visit my blog/website at **www.carolaround.com** and sign up. You'll receive a free PDF copy of my first book, *A Matter of Faith* as my gift to you.

Made in the USA
Columbia, SC
21 September 2022

67335230R00111